With Dulcimer and Double Bass

Charly Wehrle's Companions on the Trek

Carolin Schattenkirchner
Ulrich Gruber
Jochen 'Erich' Abel
Matthias 'Beeker' Bauche
Malte Jochmann
Simon Neumann
Anke Schulze

With Dulcimer and Double Bass

Trekking with Music to the Roof of the World

Charly Wehrle

With Contributions from his Companions on the Trek

*Translated from the original German
by Manfred Meurer*

PILGRIMS PUBLISHING

◆ Varanasi ◆

With Dulcimer and Double Bass
Charly Wehrle

Published by
PILGRIMS PUBLISHING

An imprint of
PILGRIMS BOOK HOUSE
B 27/98 A-8 Nawabganj Road
Durga Kund, Varanasi 221005
Phone: 91-542-2314060
Fax: 91-542-2312456
E-mail: pilgrims@satyam.net.in
Website: www.pilgrimsbooks.com

ISBN 81-7769-576-2

All photos by Charly Wehrle.
Photos on p. 12 by Malte Jochmann and p. 191 by Andi Wipper.

Layout and typesetting by
Astricks, New Delhi 110070, www.astricks.com

Printed in India at
Surya Print Process Private Limited,
9/54 Kirti Nagar Industrial Area, New Delhi 110015

For my Parents

Contents

Translator's Note

Since the English edition of this book is for an audience who are unlikely to be familiar with some of the German references presumed to be common knowledge for German readers, I felt it needed a short introduction to the background, as well as a few explanations.

When Charly Wehrle first asked me to translate this book into English, I had to give it some thought. Most of my translations have been from English to German. Although I have lived in the English-speaking world for over twenty-five years now, surrounded by literature in English, I still prefer translating into the language I grew up with, and was educated in. I do not think this is unique for most translators.

Why, then, did I decide to translate this book from German into English? Firstly, because I know Charly Wehrle and wanted to help him, and secondly, I liked the subject and the idea. I love language, music, and the mountains. This book offers the perfect combination, including a music CD.

As I read it, I felt I was following the footsteps of the trekkers, which is the next best thing to actually being there. I have not yet trekked in Nepal myself. However, I am quite familiar with the Bavarian references in the book. In my early twenties, I climbed most of the peaks of the Wetterstein and Karwendel ranges. I was crazy enough to climb the 2,000 metres from Partenkirchen to the top of the Alpspitze, in ski boots, with skis on my shoulders, when I could have taken the gondola almost halfway up. At that time, the cable car went only to the Kreuzeck. Now, a longer cable car goes as far as the Osterfelder, the snowfields below the summit wall. I went alone and was the only one on the peak. One remembers days like these, image by image, almost like a movie, the hard work and its reward, a magnificent view of 'the world' and skiing down through 'virgin' powder snow.

I have been at the Reintalanger Hut on the Partnach — this was before Charly's days, at the Knorr Hut higher up, halfway to the Zugspitze, and at the Schachenhaus, near the wooden hunting lodge of Ludwig II of Bavaria, definitely his most modest 'castle', quite unlike Neuschwanstein.

In short, it was a feeling of nostalgia that made me want to translate the book.

As far as the dominant Nepalese content is concerned, I had to do some research to make certain that I had the correct English words and spellings for names, ranging from gods and goddesses to things as mundane like Asian vegetables. I found that there were slight variations between various books and travel guides in this respect. I have tried to be consistent in the usage of the most commonly used spellings. Differences in spelling Nepalese names in German and English are not surprising, because foreign names are often spelt to suit the phonetics of a language. Thus, the Tibetan griddle-cooked bread, for instance, written *Tschappati* in German, becomes *chappati* in English, and both are pronounced in the same way. The mighty Cho Oyu, on the other hand, will always remain Cho Oyu in any language that uses the Latin alphabet. I had no access to an 'official' Nepalese map of the Himalayas, but assumed that the authors of travel guides are as 'official' as possible.

Any foreign words or names not explained within the text, would be found in the Glossary.

Any translator will acknowledge that there are culture-specific terms or phrases for which there may be no precise equivalents in many other languages. Although I was not translating Goethe or Rilke, I encountered a few problematic words, where only an approximation was possible. On the whole, I have kept the text as true as possible, trying to make it as smooth, flowing and readable as a book that has been constructed in English. Should a reader still trip, occasionally, over a stone or boulder along the path, I ask for forgiveness and appreciate suggestions. We learn everyday.

I would like to express my gratitude to Kathy See for the long hours she put into her critical reading of my English drafts, with many excellent suggestions, and for her constructive criticism.

I should say no more except for one thing: relax in your armchair, immerse yourself in an imaginative Sunday afternoon outing to the Everest, while listening to the charming music which accompanies this book on CD.

Manfred Meurer
Toronto

Author's Note
for the English Edition

The story of our musical trek has been enjoyed by many readers of the German edition, *Mit Hackbrett und Kontrabass*. I have been asked by several people over the years if an English version was available. This edition, will hopefully fulfil that demand. It would also enable me to share the story with a wider audience. For this my heartfelt thanks to Manfred Meurer for doing an excellent job of translation.

Sitting in the cosy restaurant of Pilgrims Book Shop in Kathmandu, eighteen years ago, after our musical trek, enjoying a glass of wine, it was hard to imagine that in the year 2007, Rama Nand, the owner would be publishing the English version titled *With Dulcimer and Double Bass*. I would like to thank him for taking the initiative in bringing out this edition.

Thanks are also due to Ravi Maini and his team at Surya for enhancing the quality of the photographs for this edition.

Happiness is a means to recognise truth,
for, to acquire this knowledge, the soul,
that was restless and confused,
must become pure and serene and happy.

Butön, Buddhist Philosopher,
1290–1364

Introduction

I have often wondered where my passion for travel origi-
nated from. The fact that my father taught me to read seems
to me the most obvious reason. Childhood dreams turned
into the dreams of a young man until, finally, I was bitten by
the travel bug. My hitchhiking forays to the various corners of
the Alps were only the beginning.

※

Prayer flags flapping in the wind, connecting earth with the cosmos.

When I was about to be drafted into military service, from
1967 to 1968, I applied for the mountaineers in Mittenwald,
however, for unknown reasons, I was sent to Brannenburg.

I met some climbers from Garmisch-Partenkirchen, on a climbing tour in the Swabian Alb in 1970, with whom I became good friends. They introduced me to the Werdenfels area, which I had always wanted to explore: the Wetterstein mountain range, the Stuiben Hut, Oberrein valley, as well as the Garmisch Alpine Club. My hitherto uneventful life took a decisive turn here; in one way, deep into the Wetterstein mountains, in another, far out into the world.

I made the acquaintance of Rainer and Elisabeth Pliske at the Stuiben Hut at Christmas in 1972. Rainer had his mandolin with him. With Siggi Thomasch, who accompanied him softly on his accordion, they provided the musical entertainment on Christmas Eve in our little room. This was always a very special event. During our conversation, I found out that he and his wife Elisabeth were planning to move to Persia for a longer period of time in the coming spring of 1973.

'My God, some people are really lucky!' I blurted out.

'Come and visit us,' Rainer suggested.

'And how do you suggest I do that with an empty wallet?'

'Quite simple, Charly. There is a regular bus from Munich to Tehran, run by this Europabus company in Frankfurt. They are surprisingly inexpensive, about five hundred marks for the whole trip, and it includes two meals a day.'

'Okay, Rainer, I will manage to finance that trip somehow to visit you in Persia,' I said, all gung-ho, ready to leave the next day.

Soon after Christmas, I looked up the Europabus office branch at the Munich train station for information. Indeed! This bus company existed and the trip from Munich via Istanbul to Teheran was DM 450. I had feared secretly that it would be more. My excitement about the prospects of the journey was so intense, that I experienced a permanent high during the weeks that followed.

My son Thomas was born at the end of March. However my vehement refusal to marry brought the harsh disapproval of my parents down upon me. They were not exactly pacified when I informed them of my plan, not to work the following summer. I added quickly, that this wouldn't be a problem because I would be travelling between two jobs, before moving from Rosenheim to Garmisch-Partenkirchen, where I had found a new job.

'And how will you manage financially?' my father asked.

'I will manage somehow,' I replied.

In reality I was teetering on a narrow ledge. Maintenance payments would be due, as well as my home savings plan and life insurance payments.

So I applied for a bank credit of DM 1,000. The only security I could offer was the contract for my new job, which I would be starting on 7 September.

I was determined to undertake this trip, with or without money! It was important to me. I needed to gain some distance from a profession I had learned but did not like.

My brother Siggi drove me to the Munich train station on 16 June 1973, from where the Europabus left for Asia at eight in the evening. Besides the usual luggage, I also carried climbing gear like crampons, an ice pick, and down-filled clothing. I was hoping to find an opportunity to climb the 5,672 metre high Demawend.

So here I was on my very first journey via the Balkans down towards Asia. I took a day of rest in Istanbul. I absorbed the oriental life of this city on the Bosphorus with all my senses: the Blue Mosque, Hagia Sophia, the Topkapi Palace, Galata Bridge, the Golden Horn. I became even more excited, the next day on the ferry, when I watched the minarets of Istanbul's mosques disappear in the early morning mist and, with them, Europe.

The next leg of the journey through Turkey, past Mount Ararat and into Persia, passed by like a dream. I was enchanted by Teheran, spread at the foot of the Touchal, the breathtaking sites of the city of Ghom with the golden cupolas of its mosques, the turquoise coloured minarets of Isfahan, and the beautiful gardens in Shiraz. I was fascinated by a theatre performance at ancient Persepolis, but the highlight of my whole journey was climbing the Demawend in the Elburs Mountains.

The vivid memories of this first journey, so important, if not essential, will always remain with me. Ever since those days in the summer of 1973, the culture and the simple way of life of the people of Asia hold the greatest fascination for me.

Three years later I had an opportunity to participate in an expedition to Nanga Parbat with Herrligkoffer. Wanda Rutkiewicz was the second expedition leader. The project ended in a tragedy. Sebastian Arnold from Innsbruck fell to his death and we did not reach the summit.

This journey into the interior of Asia had an enormous impact on me. The experience of being part of an expedition, the harsh and unforgiving mountains of the Karakorum, as well as the personality of Wanda Rutkiewicz, confirmed in me my desire for a freer and more independent life.

Four years later — I had in the meantime taken over the lease of a mountain hut — I travelled to Sri Lanka, the evergreen tropical island in the Indian Ocean. I was able to visit Jaffna in the extreme north, just prior to the outbreak of the separatist conflict, without any problems. This would be very dangerous now, if not impossible.

Thirteen years went by, with trips to many different countries, before I returned to Asia, this time to travel across India. The slums of Bombay, the charm of Goa, tropical Kerala and the holy city of Varanasi on the Ganges, presented me with many faces of this vast country.

I travelled by bus to Kathmandu via northern India, thus getting to know Nepal. Although I only had about two weeks, I hoped for good enough weather to spend time in the Solo Khumbu. On my way to the Lobuche and Gokyo peaks, I met Sherpa Ang Gyaltsen. A coincidental meeting turned into a very special friendship. A bridge from the Wetterstein mountains to the interior of Asia was established, born out of a deep love for this continent, that had its beginnings in the summer of 1973.

Sherpa Ang Gyaltsen

Reintalanger

Carolin Schattenkirchner

At the foot of the Zugspitze, the highest mountain in Germany, lies the Reintalanger Hut, at a height of 1,370 metres. For the last three years, I have been spending a month in the summer at this hut.

When night falls upon the Reintal, and the mountain hikers, exhausted from their day's adventures, relax in the dining room, restored by Charly's food and wine- and beer cellar, they enjoy a little live music. Charly, who manages the hut, plays the dulcimer. All other musical offerings and instruments depend on who happens to be visiting the hut at the time. Tonight it is double bass, accordion, and two guitars. As on most evenings, Sherpa Gyaltsen is also there. He comes from a Nepalese village, situated at a height of 3,440 metres at the foot of the world's highest mountain. In comparison, the mere 1,370 metres of the Reintalanger Hut seems small to me. Not even the brutally steep wall opposite the hut, with its 1,000 metres of near vertical rise, would bring it close to the height of Gyaltsen's village. To me, the gigantic proportions of the mountains surrounding his village are unimaginable. The thought alone of peaks which are 5,000, 6,000 or 8,000 metres high, instil a fear of heights in me. Standing outside the hut and letting my eyes wander about the 1,000 metres of

Reintalanger Hut — A piece of Nepal in the Wetterstein.

wall from top to bottom, I have to tilt my head pretty far back
to be able to see the peak, and wonder if I would break my
neck trying to look up to the peaks of the gigantic mountains
of Nepal.

Gyaltsen tells me that there is one Nepalese word for
mountain and one for hill. To my question, what would he
call this wall, he answers with a mischievous smile: 'hill'.

One night, when it was especially nice and everyone was
happy, with Gyaltsen particularly enjoying our music, Charly
suggested his idea: 'When Gyaltsen turns sixty, we will all play
for his birthday in his village in Nepal!'

I have to laugh. The idea to me is as unimaginable as the
giant mountains of Nepal . . .

'Carry my double bass on a ten days foot march, past the
last bus station, to the little village of Namche Bazar? Not I!'

And yet, six months later, in February 1998, the year when
Gyaltsen would turn sixty, Charly rang up: 'This coming
December we are off to Nepal. You are coming along, aren't
you?'

Stone Man at Reintalanger.

One after the other, he persuaded Malte and Simon, two guitarists, Erich, the accordion player, and Beeker, a drummer. They were old friends, who could often be found at the Reintalanger Hut. In addition, he engaged the cameramen Andi and Ebi, to document the journey of the wayfaring musicians. This would now make us an eight-member team. In Nepal, Sherpa Gyaltsen would join us with six carriers. In early January, a further member of the Reintal crew would join us: Anke from Berlin.

Resham Firiri

Another mountain holiday season is nearing its end, meaning that I am a year older. My birthday usually coincides with the closing of the hut. If it happens to be on a weekend, the house is full of friends; if it is during the week, it usually turns out to be a very quiet and cosy day. The night before, we stay up until midnight in order to greet the New Year by celebrating.

Every year, my helpers come up with a special surprise for my birthday, as is the case this year. Beginning in the early evening, I am prevented from entering the kitchen, so I will not, by accident, come upon something that might be meant as a surprise for me. Eventually, just before midnight, I am allowed to leave the guest dining hall. My friends shove me out of the door.

Below, by the creek, the picnic tables are standing in a group, as usual one of them is decorated with a lot of tea lights, arranged in the figure '49'. They glow far in the darkness of the night. A wonderful idea from my creative friends. I am touched.

Carolin and Erich, the camera team for our Nepal expedition, Ebi and Andi, as well as a few other friends, arrive at the hut the next morning. Even Anke, who should be studying for her Masters degree, is there. After a cosy afternoon coffee hour, we indulge in a superb lamb roast and good wine in the evening. After that, Matthias 'Beeker' Bauche, Carolin and Erich entertain us with jazzy pieces, and then all of us play Bavarian folk tunes.

In between, I am occupied with unwrapping birthday presents. One of them is an envelope that I open curiously. Three pages of handwritten sheet music surface. On close scrutiny, I recognise Nepalese music, arranged by Erich.

I study the pages for quite a while, with Erich watching me.

'Does this mean I have to learn these pieces for our trip?' I ask, a bit apprehensively.

'Charly, if possible, by November. Please, be so kind. These are three of the most popular pieces of Nepalese folk music. You will see, they will be a resounding success,' Erich tries to cheer me up.

'I will try, even though I feel stretched to the limit at the moment. Don't be disappointed if I don't make it, Erich.'

'Look here, Charly, I will play them for you. First *Resham Firiri*, number one on the hit parade in Nepal.' He plays the tune on his accordion and I fall in love with it instantly. But, *Nepali 2* and *Nepali 3* also have a lot of character; especially *Nepali 2* which with its minor chords, sounds very melancholic to me. Erich had encountered these tunes with an acquaintance in Kathmandu, and has arranged them especially for our group for accordion, tenor horn, dulcimer, percussion and three guitars. As soon as the hut is made ready for winter, I register for dulcimer lessons with Marianne Kirch in Munich-Haidhausen. I feel compelled to accomplish the task. Soon, I feel quite comfortable and play without the slightest apprehension, I look forward to the first group rehearsals at the Alpine Museum in Munich. Erich, who plays with two different bands in Stuttgart, with Carolin and Beeker, as well as solo, has to put up with us amateurs. During those days, he is quite stressed and sometimes criticizes us impatiently, but his criticism is objective and constructive; without it, we would not have progressed as we have. And so all of us go along with him.

Three weeks later, we meet for the main rehearsal in Bernhausen, near Stuttgart, where he tells us again: 'practice,

Rehearsal at the Anchor restaurant.

practice, practice.' Erich handles us with an iron grip. We will present two short concerts at the weekend in the Anchor, an alternative pub in Bernhausen, above which Erich and Carolin live.

In the afternoon we set the stage. We dress up a bit for the evening. Then at 9 p.m. the trumpet sounds. The Anchor is bursting at the seams, blue with cigarette smoke, and it is unbearably hot. Although I have practised and learned a lot, my nerves play tricks with me. Not even tranquillisers help. The critical passage in *Resham Firiri* goes better than expected, but I goof at the solo part in *Nepali 3*. Nevertheless, the audience applauds and finds the Nepalese pieces 'fantastic'. On the following evening, the Anchor is just as packed as the night before, and my nervousness has completely vanished. We play in perfect unison and are ecstatically happy when the audience demands *Resham Firiri* as an encore.

In Search of a Case
for the Double Bass

In the beginning, Carolin is, in principle, dead against carrying a double bass into the Himalaya. We have been discussing the pros and cons for a long time. In the end though, I convince Carolin. The reason I give is, that it is the double bass which will represent the centrepiece of our band, and that it makes for good photos and is extremely important for our filming because of its uniqueness in the environment, convinces her. I don't know why, but I like the warm sound of the double bass and its ability to create a homely atmosphere. It would be good for us to have it along on our trek.

Carolin finally gives in. 'All right, but *my* bass stays here!'

'And my old treasure from the hut will also stay here,' I agree. 'It is much too delicate.'

Indeed, because of the extreme temperature changes during the winter months, it is quite a problem to travel with a wooden instrument. A double bass could crack in conditions like that. Luckily, there are fibreglass basses and, better yet, Carolin's teacher owns one. It is relatively new, and not inexpensive. Fortunately, she sympathises with us and lends us the bass on the condition that we take extremely good care of it, particularly with its transport. A regular bass case is too thin and fragile for air transport as well as at high altitudes and in extreme cold.

So, where do we find a case for a bass? I make a phone call to the Geigenbau-Museum in Mittenwald, where a friendly

Carolin with the venerable Double Bass at a
traditional evening of music at the Reintalanger.

employee is of great help. 'Just go to Michael Krahmer, here in town, the double bass maker. He leases such boxes for transport.' 'Thanks a million.' Off I go to Mittenwald, through the Werdenfels country under deep snow, in search of the recommended craftsman. Eventually, I find the workshop. An alert young man welcomes me. I explain our project to him, as well as the fact that our financial situation is already quite stressed. The explanation seems unnecessary, because Michael Krahmer is so excited about our idea and the whole project that he volunteers to lend us one of two cases he has presently stored in his garage. I am very grateful for his kindness to offer this as a contribution to our musical expedition, without charge. Normally these giant stiff polyester coffins are used by orchestras, like the Münchner Philharmoniker, for their world tours. The last trip of our box was to Korea.

In his picturesque workshop, overflowing with basses and bass parts, where a journeyman is occupied with the restoration of an old double bass, we have an animated conversation about our planned Himalayan adventure. He wants to come up to the hut for a visit in the summer.

Only with pushing and shoving can I fit the oversized case into my Opel. The neck just barely fits between the two front seats. On my way back to Ohlstadt, I say to myself, 'What a lucky duck you are!' But I am already thinking of the enormous overweight problem we will have, which will be in the neighbourhood of 100 kg. This case alone is 50 kg. My dulcimer is 20 kg, and then there are the cameras etc. Again we are lucky. The sympathetic airline gives us an excess baggage allowance of 80 kg.

Departure

The Werdenfels countryside lies buried under snow. It is the morning of 4 December, I leave Ohlstadt with mixed feelings. I am extremely excited and curious about the next few weeks. It is the first time since the Nanga Parbat expedition in 1976, that I will be travelling with a large group. On almost every major trip, in the past and on various continents, I have been completely on my own. What if a member of the group becomes ill, or if we do not get along, or if we encounter problems with our carriers, or if bad weather crosses our plans altogether? It might not be that simple to guide eight individuals safely, through all kinds of possible problems that might arise on such an adventure.

However, as soon as I close the door behind me, I feel detached from all everyday responsibilities and the good feelings about our adventure prevail. Aside from my general joy of life, I think, a little shot of naivety has always turned out to protect me in a way.

A heavy snow squall turns the road into a slide. The radio station, Bayern 3, plays soft pop music, interrupted by the road report: the Munich-Nuremberg-Frankfurt Autobahn is partially snow covered; then again, the familiar Bayern 3 jingle. Simon is expecting me impatiently. I can see that he is completely in the grip of travel jitters and can barely contain his excitement. The rear view mirror is useless now. With Simon's luggage, my Opel is packed to the roof. I can barely see my companion. He is trapped in his seat by the double bass case. We are taking turns driving en route to Frankfurt. It is snowing less now. Simon likes loud and hard music but I am allowed to switch to Bayern 2 for the mountaineering programme. At Wertheim/Main, we hit the evening rush hour, which delays our arrival at Werner's, my eldest brother's place in the Rodgau. 'Hello, globetrotters!' he greets us. Hilde, my sister-in-law, invites us to stay for supper, but we want to get back on the road, since it has started to snow more heavily now. Somehow, we manage to squeeze my nephew Klaus into the interior of the car. We need him to take the car back to his place. Before reaching Frankfurt Airport, we do some serious skidding with the car. The unloading in the underground garage takes a while: backpacks, sea bags, guitar, dulcimer, and finally the bass case, which has little casters for easier transport. As we negotiate glass and sliding doors with the bulky monster, we cause some head-shaking among the other passengers.

Our meeting point is the check-in counter of Royal Nepal Airlines. Simon and I are the first ones to arrive at 9 p.m. Everyone else is on time; first Carolin, Erich and Beeker, then Malte and Ebi, then the last one, Andi. Our faces radiate the kind of curious suspense that is so much part of the tingling ambience of an airport. Everyone has acquired a short haircut and are wearing new down jackets — blue, yellow, red and black.

Instead of a punctual departure at 11:05 p.m., we get treated with a coupon for dinner at the Chinese restaurant at the airport. We pass the time eating, sitting relaxed in a corner reading or napping, until we are asked to check-in. Thank God, we have no problem with the luggage. By three o'clock, everything is stowed away, passport control and security checks are behind us and we are now eagerly awaiting the boarding signal. Finally, just past 4 a.m., we board, and a friendly stewardess greets us at the door with a 'Good morning! *Namaste!*'

The first daily newspapers are distributed. We can spread

View from the plane on the flight to Kathmandu.

out over the whole plane. There are very few passengers, which suits us perfectly. We can lie flat across the seats and get a good rest. At 5 a.m., the Nepalese plane finally takes off, in the direction of the Balkans, Asia, to the Far East. We experience a wonderful daylight flight with clear views of Turkey and Mt. Ararat; later, bizarre desert landscapes and the gigantic volcano of the more than 5,000 metre high Demawend in Iran. My thoughts trail back to earlier years. It's incredible to think that it was twenty-five years ago when I climbed this peak with Rainer and Elisabeth Pliske, on a gorgeous sunny day in July 1973, each of us suffering excruciating headaches, but easily rewarded with a most magnificent view across the immensity of Asia. There is a special place in my memory for the beautiful dark red Oriental poppies at the foot of the giant volcano, and for the white donkey which carried our equipment to the bivouac.

Arrival

Our Airbus touches down softly at Tribhuvan International Airport, Kathmandu. We have already prepared our hand baggage and are a bit nervous, particularly Malte, Simon, Carolin, Beeker and Ebi, who have not been to Nepal before. Will Sherpa Gyaltsen be there to meet us with a few helpers? We have not heard from him for a while.

'Ladies and gentlemen, we have arrived in Kathmandu. The local time is 7 p.m. Please keep your seat belt fastened until the aircraft arrives at the final parking position,' the soothing voice of the head stewardess entices us. As we leave the plane, she bids us goodbye, with her hands folded as in prayer, and a reverential *'Namaste'*. Simple greeting ceremonies like this are already evidence of the magic of this exotic country. I feel joyful anticipation, a sense of freedom, just like the last time. Although it is warm, I feel a shiver running down my spine as I walk down the gangway.

Curious glances follow our double bass box, which we have stuffed with clothes, in Frankfurt. The security and control staff want to scrutinise every single piece of luggage and are surprised by the 'big guitar', as they call it, which appears among our expedition equipment. They enquire in detail what we are planning to do with all the instruments; then we are allowed to pass the customs officers. The arrivals hall is teeming with people, dark-skinned, wealthy looking merchants in dark grey suits, elegant women in beautiful saris and tourists with an outdoor look — a colourful mix. Here and there are a few Sikhs, recognisable by their artfully wrapped turbans, many of them awaiting travellers from Pokhara, New Delhi or Varanasi. Outside there is a crowd, noses and hands flattened against the glass panes, children, taxi drivers, women dressed in bright colours, men in drab frocks and *Dukus*. Somewhere in the chaos, we discover Sherpa Gyaltsen in his blue Patagonia sweater. He is beaming from ear to ear and waving to us.

'Taxi, Taxi!' We are being overwhelmed from all sides, as we drag our baggage into the open. An army of arms is trying to pull pieces of luggage from our hands: 'I help you! I help you!' Luckily, Gyaltsen is right there, and with great joy and excitement, and 'How are you?' and 'I am fine, and you?' we greet and hug each other. We have to drag our luggage to a VW bus which belongs to Gyaltsen's nephew, through a swarm of people. We are crowded by protesting cab drivers who underbid one another. Undisturbed, we keep loading our luggage, one by one, into the bus. The last piece, the 'big guitar', has to go on the rack on top of the roof. We are holding on tight to our hand luggage. Gyaltsen's nephew has barely enough room behind the wheel of the overcrowded vehicle. We take two taxis, in which we sit cramped, elbow to elbow, and immediately break out into a sweat. It is so warm, such an extreme contrast to the winter temperatures in Germany, to which we are still accustomed. As I glance over at Malte and Simon, who are with me in the taxi, I recognise the same longing and joyful anticipation I felt when I passed checkpoint into Kathmandu, one late evening in February 1993, hitchhiking on a truck.

I first met the two when they came as students to the Reintalanger Hut, four years ago. Simon camped outside, on a nearby meadow in his tent, and tried to be self-sufficient. That was very important to him. He hardly ever spoke. I liked him, though. Bit by bit, he became more sociable, an excellent co-worker and a loyal friend. His modest and quiet ways will be a great asset for our team. Malte also worked regularly at the hut. With his sociable, but unimposing and charming manner, he fits so well into the community spirit of life at the hut, that I cannot imagine it without him.

The suburbs of the metropolis do not seem to have changed much during the six years. There are hardly any street lights, only the occasional faint lantern, tight curvy asphalt streets with potholes; and the doors of the taxi rattle to the beat of a Nepalese song, moaning from a dying car radio.

Occasionally, a group of people scurries to the side into the dark.

The picture changes in the vicinity of the Royal Palace, as the street leads into the tourist centre Thamel, along with the level of street noise. As if one had suddenly been transported into a fairy tale! A flotilla of roaring tricycles, tuk-tuks, are whizzing by between cabs. Numerous colourful bicycle rickshaws, with their slender operators, are part of the scene.

The narrow lanes and alleys are crowded with tourists from every corner of the world, to a point where we seem to be hopelessly stuck in the traffic. Our Nepal novices are fascinated by the exotic magic of the place, the fantastically decorated storefronts, the glittering alleys of Thamel. And I, as well, am exuberant with joy to be here again after six years.

'Which hotel?' the cab driver asks. 'Hotel Shree Antu near Seven Corners,' Gyaltsen answers. Two more turns past Pilgrims Book House, at the end of a row of countless souvenir shops, the VW bus and the two taxis stop in the driveway of the hotel Shree Antu. We are very pleased with it. Gyaltsen has chosen it for us, after critical comparison with several accommodations. He seems to have found the best one as far as location, price and ambience are concerned. After the procedure of unloading everything again, Diren, the friendly young manager of the hotel, welcomes us, impeccably dressed in pressed trousers, white shirt, tie and black leather jacket.

Culture Shock

Carolin Schattenkirchner

Today, nine months after the decision to travel to Nepal with our instruments, we disembark from the aeroplane at Kathmandu. After small formalities with customs officers — the only interesting object is the coffin-like structure which housed my double bass during the flight — we leave the airport building.

Outside it is like a zoo. We have a hard time keeping our eight-member team together in this crowd, especially with the pile of baggage: one dulcimer, one double bass, two guitars, one accordion, one tenor horn, one drum, seven big backpacks, one small backpack (this one is mine; I am very lazy and have only packed the most essential items), one big metal box — what is in it? Oh yes, Charly's office. There is also a video camera, a film camera, a tripod, and four big sea bags.

There, among the crowd is our friend Gyaltsen. The welcome is brief but heartfelt. We have caused a minor disturbance and attracted a major crowd, interested in our luggage. Therefore, Gyaltsen is in a hurry to stow everything, including us, as fast as possible into a VW bus and a sort of Range Rover. There are many helping hands and we are getting nervous because we are starting to lose control. There are lots of street urchins, who are not Gyaltsen's helpers. When we realise this, suddenly it is not quite clear anymore whether we still have all our pieces of luggage together. As swiftly as we can, we leave the airport in our taxis, a place that seems like one big turmoil to us newcomers.

After an exciting drive (left side traffic rules here — most of the time, that is!), we arrive at the hotel that Gyaltsen has found for us. The first thing to do is to sort out our luggage and, we nearly have a heart attack; the backpack of Ebi, our cameraman, is missing. A small detachment of the team races straight back to the airport to find the culprit. False alarm! The backpack is safe and sound at the luggage reception. We are all relieved and happy and enjoy the rest of the evening with tea on the veranda of the hotel.

In the morning, I dare to go on a first excursion through the quarter; cars, bicycles, rickshaws, and other two-wheelers pass and crisscross each other in the wildest manner, all ringing their bells at the same time. Into the traffic chaos plunges a mass of colourfully dressed people, of seemingly various tribes. All of the throbbing everyday life seems to take place in the street. A tailor is sitting under a tree with his sewing machine, working on a suit for a client, who is sitting next to him. Right beside him, a butcher is in the process of spreading pieces of meat on a plastic sheet. A fishmonger is sitting on his heels in a wooden shack among his fish; next to him, for a few rupees, you can eat spaghetti, which is served by dirty fingers directly from the pot. Not far away lies a dead dog in a narrow lane, and six- to eight-year-old street children are searching through a pile of rubbish for something edible. Further below, on the banks of the river, lies an object wrapped in an orange cloth. A dead body! A group of drummers next to it are playing peculiar, never-heard rhythms. And amongst all this activity I see a man without legs. He is moving with the help of his hands, which are slipped into sandals, begging at the same time. I keep discovering the most beautiful houses and palaces with exquisite decorations and carvings: temple after temple — each one more beautiful and bigger than the other, *stupas*, monasteries and other sacred places. Adrenaline- and culture-shocked from impressions and encounters, I make my way back to the hotel. In the afternoon, we play music on the hotel roof and discuss the final details necessary for our ten-day trek. We only have one more day in Kathmandu, the city whose charm has already taken me prisoner. I can hardly wait to be back here after three weeks for further journeys of discovery. For now I am looking forward to tomorrow, when our musical trek will start towards the highest mountain on earth. There, I shall see if I can bend my head back far enough in order to be able to see the peaks of these gigantic mountains.

Mobile fruit vendors in Kathmandu.

Kathmandu

I wake up to a nasal voice. I strain my ears — and again, I hear this peculiar sound. From the balcony I look down onto the street. A young boy, walking the streets barefeet, is signalling to the residents that he is collecting empty bottles. He is wearing an old blanket, against the cold, and carrying a jute sack. Again this strange nasal sound. He is probably one of the first to populate the street aside from the newspaper carriers. Soon the tuk-tuks roar through the narrow street, followed shortly by the rattling of shutters, as the stores open for business. I go back to bed and doze off again. Simon and Malte are still in a deep sleep, as if anaesthetised.

At about eight o'clock, I start off for the Pumpernickel, which was my favourite café in Thamel back in 1993. At the next major intersection, there are plenty of cars. 'Taxi! Taxi, Mister?' A few metres further: 'Rickshaw, Mister, rickshaw, very cheap!' The day has fully awakened. To my right is a music store, from which the sound of an Indian sitar contributes to the atmosphere. On the left side are a bakery, a café, a money-changer, and many trekking agencies. I pass Pilgrims Book House, probably the best known bookstore in Kathmandu. Ahead of me I see the first terrace café. At the next intersection, from where the main street leads to Chetrapati, a bookstore is ready for business packed with postcards, maps, and the latest daily newspapers: *Gorkha Patra* in Nepali, *Rising Nepal* and *Kathmandu Post* in English. *The Indian Express, USA Today* and the *Herald Tribune*, the most important international papers here, are also available. There are magazines in

Nepali, English, French and German. Although Kathmandu is not a very large city, compared to other large cities of the world, it boasts a great international representation. Already in the early morning, the streets are crowded with tourists, bald-headed characters, beautiful women, middle-aged couples who enjoy travelling and life in general.

'Very cheap rickshaws here,' 'give me rupees' from the other side. The beggars have a prime season. One often sees wretched figures indeed, those who live literally in the gutter, without legs, blind, or leprous. Children are sent to the streets to sell junk of all sorts. Their main business is selling small boxes of Tiger Balm, which are easy to sell and make a light souvenir for the tourists to take along. On the left is a store with artful *thangkas*. Based on ancient scrolls, these rolled-up pictures are painted on fine cotton or silk to which a base of a mixture of chalk, glue and indigo is applied. An application of duck egg white with water, gives the base a fine lustre. The outlines of the mostly Buddhist figures are drawn with charcoal and a very fine brush before the colours are applied with

Rickshaws dominate the view in the alleys of Kathmandu.

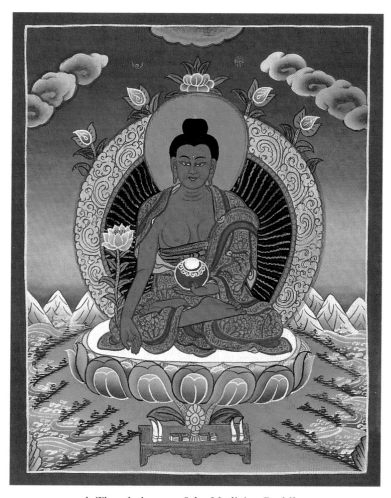

A *Thangka* image of the Medicine Buddha
(Skt: *Bhaisajyaguru,* Tib: *Sangye Menla,* Chin: *Yaoshi-fo,* Jap: *Yakushi*).
According to ancient knowledge, merely seeing the Medicine Buddha,
chanting or hearing his name is beneficial.

Tibetan images of the Medicine Buddha usually show the left hand
holding a blooming myrobalan plant. Tibetan medicine recognises three
basic types of illness whose root causes are conflicting emotions: passion,
aggression, and ignorance. Myrobalan (*Phyllanthus emblica*) or arura is the
only herb in the Tibetan pharmacopoeia that aids in healing each of these.
This is the power of the Buddha of Healing, who has the vision to see the
true cause of any affliction, whether spiritual, physical or psychological, and
the power to alleviate it. It is believed that meditating on the Medicine Buddha can help decrease illness, both physical and mental, and suffering.

a warm thin glue mix. The work is shared by apprentices and Masters, depending on experience and proficiency.

The Pumpernickel café is probably one of the best known and oldest meeting places for Westerners in Thamel. The interior is relatively simple, with plenty of wooden banquettes and, in the centre, a hardly to be missed bulletin board. Notices range from a missing travel companion to ski poles that someone wants to sell. The garden is the actual heart of the Pumpernickel, a long, narrow pathway which has been turned into a garden café. Fragments of conversations float through the air. Here are trekkers, hippies, Japanese; a young woman who is studying it with her partner, looks Tibetan. Wherever there is a spot without a table, bamboo and rhododendron create the impression of a jungle, enhanced by the twitter of swarms of tame birds, picking breadcrumbs off the ground and tables. At the buffet you can get the best cinnamon rolls in Kathmandu, plus anything you could possibly want for breakfast: milk, coffee, tea, fresh-pressed orange juice, muesli with fresh fruit, croissants, wheat bread, yoghurt. Six or seven local waiters are moving quickly to fill the requests of the international clientele. This is a place to dream, to make friends and business contacts, to read, to update one's diary, a place to relax. I have an appointment with Gyaltsen for 10 a.m. Rarely have I met someone as punctual as he is. He is reliability itself.

'Good morning, sir', he greets me.

'Good morning, Gyaltsen, did you sleep well?'

Over a cup of tea we discuss the agenda for the day. Most important are the permits for the Sagarmatha National Park. It is impossible to travel without them to Namche Bazar, Gyaltsen's home. Without them, the checkpoint in Mondzo would, no doubt, send us straight back to Kathmandu. The Nepalese are very strict as far as documents are concerned.

We stroll back to the Shree Antu through the activities of the morning, which have escalated by now. 'Come inside, mister, just look!' someone calls over to us. Gyaltsen laughs across his whole weather-beaten face.

Everyone has got up in the meantime. 'Folks, I need your passports. Gyaltsen will take me to the Immigration Office for the permits.' We rush off by tuk-tuk to the tourist bureau, while our friends head for the next garden café for breakfast. At 1 p.m. we will meet again on the balcony of the Shree Antu to play music for an hour.

Our mini-taxi tuk-tuk's through the heavy morning traffic, taking the occasional short cut or skilfully avoiding an ox cart. I notice some women in colourful saris who are wearing their adornments like a second skin.

The Immigration Office looks like a bazaar. I had no idea that there would be such a big crowd of trekkers. Do we wait, or take advantage of one of the young locals who will do all the paperwork and get the necessary approvals for us, at seven dollars per person? We decide to avoid the crowd and have our papers delivered later in the afternoon to the hotel by one of the young fellows.

We have set up our instruments on the the second floor balcony of the Shree Antu. Erich leads the beat and we play from our Bavarian repertoire, the *Schoenauer Boarischer*, a Berchtesgaden 2/4 folk tune, which sounds quite catchy. The first piece is barely over when we receive roaring applause from the other balconies and terraces. We are delighted and pleased and Gyaltsen is very proud of us. After all, it is his sixtieth birthday, for which we have made the journey to Nepal. The chirping of the birds, noise from the cars, the loud voices below and Bavarian folk music make a very rare and cheerful mixture. Andi and Ebi have prepared their cameras for first takes.

I had met Andi for the first time four years ago, during a film shoot at the Reintalanger Hut. He is an electrical engineer by trade, but keeps flirting with filmmaking. We did not know Ebi, a friend of the Stuttgarters, before the trip. He is a cameraman by profession and has volunteered to document our musical trek.

During the daytime, when temperatures are almost like a summer day, there is no problem with an out-of-tune guitar or dulcimer. Playing the Nepali pieces for the first time since we arrived, we put all our emotion into *Resham Firiri*. We seem to melt into the exoticism of Nepal and feel we could hardly have a better initiation.

A little later, we are invited for tea at the house of Gyaltsen's sister Dolma and her husband, Nima Tenzing. Nima was one of the most successful and favoured Sherpas for high altitude mountaineering in the sixties. He was on Dhaulagiri with the Swiss expedition in 1960; with the first ascent to the 7,000 metre high Pumori in 1962, and a member of Norman Dyrenfurth's team in 1963, which reached the peak of Mount Everest over the West Ridge. He was honoured by a reception with John F. Kennedy, shortly before his tragic assassination. Nima and his wife own a house in the Lazimpat quarter, which only wealthy people can afford. Ferocious dogs guard their estate.

Inside the house, there is solid furniture. Tibetan rugs and colourful *thangkas* provide a cosy and comfortable atmosphere. There have been frequent disagreements between both of them in the past, possibly due to rivalry or jealousy. But that is a thing of the past and, for Nima, it is an honour that Gyaltsen visits him with his friends from Germany, who will be presenting a private concert as well.

Erich's ingenious idea to study the three Nepali songs at home, gives us, for the second time today, great prestige. Nima and his family really enjoy the music. We are having a wonderful tea hour. I like the features of the men and study the faces of the two Sherpas repeatedly, rippled with laughter lines, and the gold crowns on the otherwise snow-white teeth. The dogs in the courtyard are announcing visitors. It is time for us to leave and thank all for the invitation. Gyaltsen remains.

We have great fun on our first evening at the Seven Corners, a nightclub, which is just around the corner from our hotel. The excellent food, the dancing of the local girls and women and, in particular the performance of a transvestite, are a big hit with everyone. The style of the nightclub, with sparsely dressed entertainers, seems ahead of its time even in modern Kathmandu.

At Miss Hawley's

While Durbar Marg is dominated by offices of the major airlines and mostly expensive shops and hotels, the Dilli Bazaar offers Asian everyday life with its merchants and clients haggling over prices. The streets remind me of those in Colombo, Sri Lanka and Kolkata. New houses behind bamboo scaffolding, older brick buildings, never plastered, alternate with grey and dusty houses and a variety of shops at street level. Next to an electronics shop is a general store, exuding a strong smell of soap. A furniture store advertises modern king-size beds; next to it is a display of tools, tin kettles, wire drums, locks and more. Young women in saris are searching for their favourite patterns in the fabric stalls. A fruit vendor with a wide basket on his bicycle offers tangerines and bananas, as motor scooters, buses, rattling taxis and black-and-yellow tuk-tuks drive by.

Smog is hanging in the street. Even if it increases in the coming years, life here will go on the same way it always has. The chaotic electricity cables above will be the same and people will crowd the streets in the same relaxed attitude, pretty, slender women in saris carrying their children, the old man in the shabby jacket that hides his worn dhoti, businessmen in suits and ties, students in blue uniforms, the cheerful sadhu walking behind with his tin can, the cab driver who buys the latest edition of the *Kathmandu Post* at the kiosk, stray dogs searching out sunny spots. Outdated posters on the brick walls will just be covered with new ones.

The houses are one-storey brown structures with numerous

Sadhus at Durbar Square.

small windows, held in place by wooden frames. Among all the buildings, street noise and activities, and among the fruit and vegetable markets, goat vendors and rickshaw drivers, the various tribes of Nepal meet without taking notice of the fact that Rai is next to Newar, Tamang next to Chetri, Magar side by side with Thakali, Gurung with Sherpa.

Set back a little from the busy street and brick structures, is a white house with straight walls, which can easily be missed. Through the doorless access one can look into the garden with rows of bright orange-coloured marigolds in clay pots and trees with citrus fruit which provide comfortable shade during the hot and sunny days. To the right of the entrance, a brass plate with black letters announces 'Himalaya Trust – Honorary Consul of New Zealand – Miss Elizabeth Hawley'. So this is where she lives, Miss Hawley, the chronicler of all Himalayan expeditions. Andi Wipper had asked for an audience. Gyaltsen, Ebi and I accompany him.

An elderly man, frail, with fine features, who looks Indian, asks us whom we are looking for. While Andi explains that we have an appointment with Miss Hawley, the brass bells signal that we are to enter. The polite servant guides us up a narrow, dark, polished wooden staircase and knocks softly.

Miss Hawley stands in front of us, slightly stooped. Her expression is matter-of-fact, a bit edgy, with thin lips and grey hair. She is seventy-five.

She still dedicates her time to Himalayan expeditions, just as she did in the sixties when she came to Nepal as a news correspondent for *Reuters*. She reported on mountaineers and expeditions in Nepal, and later also on those in Tibet. Although she did not climb herself, she became an expert in the field, always keeping the right critical distance, necessary to report objectively. None of the larger expeditions would neglect to pay their respects to Miss Hawley before departing for Base Camp.

'Hello, gentlemen, come in,' she welcomes all of us. Andi takes over the conversation because he speaks English fluently. We sit across from her writing desk, on a large sofa. I quickly scan the room. Everything is of good quality and very tasteful — furniture, carpets, pictures. Piles of books and magazines, as well as photos on display, suggest a rich life. Andi hands her an autographed copy of my book *Wände – Grate – Dome* (*Walls – Ridges – Domes*), which she accepts gracefully and with delight. Andi talks about Gyaltsen's previous expeditions and how our friendship with him came about. Then he explains the purpose of our present journey. Miss Hawley is not a little surprised. Her comment is: 'It sure is something different,' and she offers help. With her permission, Andi sets up his camera for some shooting. I use the opportunity to ask Miss Hawley if she had ever met Wanda Rutkiewicz.

'Oh yes, certainly! She often came to visit me. An extraordinary climber and a very charming woman. It was a terrible loss when she did not return from the Kangchenjunga.'

'I knew Wanda quite well, too.'

'How did you meet her?'

'I was with her on the south side of the Nanga Parbat in 1976, on the Toni Kinshofer path. Wanda was the second leader of the expedition. The expedition turned out to be quite tragic when the Austrian Sebastian Arnold fell to his death, but in spite of that, it was a good time.'

'Did you reach the summit?' Miss Hawley asks.

'No, after the accident we returned, although Wanda, Danuta Wuch and Dr Janosz would have liked to go on. That was really the only disagreement we had during the entire expedition.'

She shows us a newspaper article of that time. Then she is occupied with thoughts of the Everest drama of 1996. 'That was a shocking, terrible disaster.' She shakes her head. 'Rob Hall and Scott Fischer were here with me before they left for Everest.' For a while there is a heavy silence.

Then, almost abruptly, our hostess asks: 'Did you say you still had to get your bus tickets? You must excuse me now, I have another important appointment.' The hour had passed by like a shot. We thank her and she shakes everyone's hands with a friendly, 'Have a good time' and dismisses us back into the tumult of Kathmandu.

A tuk-tuk takes us swiftly to the Dechenling garden restaurant, not far from Thamel. The owner of this classy place, which is hidden in a side street, is Phintso, a business-minded Bhutanese. Giant deciduous trees form a canopy above the dinner tables. A little blue sky penetrates the green cover here and there. The waiters who serve us are composed and well dressed. Klaus Wanger arrives with two young men who are hauling a big piece of machinery. A generator for our cameramen; we cannot expect to have access to electricity everywhere. I lift it and get a shock! The thing weighs 25 kg easily.

Klaus is a certified mountaineer and guide, and the Nepal coordinator for the Deutscher Alpen-Verein (DAV) Summit

Club. He is known to be reliable. I had asked him for assistance by phone from Germany. We pay the Nepali 5,000 rupees and the monster is ours. Somehow I have the feeling we won't need it and I am embarrassed to impose this weight on a porter, even for a minute. Gyaltsen disagrees. He knows what porters have to be able to handle and tries to convince me that I should not worry about it, but rather, watch the time. We still have to get our tickets for tomorrow's bus trip to Jiri before closing time.

The bus terminal, Amika Yatayat, is very busy. Groups of people huddle together, with boxes, backpacks, bags and the typical *dokos*, are waiting for their departure. We have to cross the parking area which is littered with rubbish, past screaming children and pushy vendors who want to sell us fresh deep-fried *momos*. The queues do not worry Gyaltsen. He talks to the people in shabby frocks behind the wired windows. I catch words like Jiri and rupees. Sure, we would have been able to find our way around in Kathmandu without Sherpa Gyaltsen, but the fact that he speaks the language certainly makes it easier for us.

We have to be here tomorrow, by 6 a.m. at the latest, with our luggage.

Relaxed, because now everything is arranged, we return to Thamel.

Gyaltsen continues on to Nima Tenzing's house. I absorb the busy evening atmosphere of Thamel once more, before I stroll into the hotel, where everyone is occupied with the packing of their backpacks.

Into the Solo Khumbu

In my dream I hear . . . no, it is not a dream, Malte's alarm clock. Half asleep, I feel around for my flashlight and glasses. I look at my wristwatch; it is just minutes before 5 a.m. We will have to get up at this inhuman hour for the next few weeks. With some urgency, I shake the others awake. For sleepyheads like Elbi, Erich and Carolin, this is pure torture. Diren, the hotel manager, makes tea for us, still in his pyjamas. The Shree Antu is, compared with hotels like the Shanker or Annapurna, really just a pension, a very nice old building with perhaps fifteen rooms. The kitchen is a dive.

Diren came here from the countryside and he is happy to have his job, even though it pays only 2,000 rupees a month, about forty US dollars. There is fierce competition among those come to seek work in Kathmandu. To us, prices here are almost embarrassingly low. The Nepalese must think that all tourists are wealthy citizens. All the more admirable then is the fact that Diren manages to always look impeccable in his simple suit; he gives the hotel a touch of class. All other employees, even those with the lowest jobs, are cleanly and properly dressed, which, in this environment, looks almost surreal. We feel extremely comfortable at the Shree Antu.

The taxis, which we ordered the night before, arrive. In the dim light of the courtyard, assisted occasionally by a flashlight, we load all the original luggage, plus solar lamps and the monstrous generator. We all have another cup of tea, on the run. We want to get to the bus station as soon as possible.

Kathmandu's streets are still peaceful at this early hour.

Only the odd bicycle rickshaw is waiting for a customer, with the owner's sitting in the customer's seat, wrapped in a warm blanket, looking half asleep and cold.

We reach the station in no time at all. Hard to believe that, although still dark, there are masses of local commuters waiting to board the various buses. The scene is almost ghostlike. Sparsely dressed figures around a few campfires, along with streaks of flashlight, create a spooky dance of shadows and silhouettes.

Without much ado, Andi climbs on to the roof of the bus, to safely tie down our luggage, while we keep on the alert in the dark. It is in the bus stations where interesting-looking luggage sometimes disappears without a trace. Most globe-trotters are very much aware of this. And indeed, in Jiri we would discover that two of our solar lamps were missing. It is possible though, that we simply left them in the trunks of one of the taxis.

The engine of our bus, No. 52, has been running for nearly half an hour. The old diesel motor probably has to warm up. Holding our numbered tickets, we finally find our seats. The left row has two seats, the one on the right has three seats. Unfortunately, the three seats have hardly more space than the two seats, and we are all seated in the triple row. This does not look promising!

Finally, we hear the grinding sound of the transmission shifting into gear, and we are on our way. Soon we pass the outskirts of Kathmandu. The morning rush hour traffic with its smog lies behind us. An almost clear blue sky lets us, for now, ignore the cramped accommodation. The driver turns the radio to Indian music. Soon the locals are singing along with the exotic tunes. We are driving through magnificent rhododendron forests, then terraced fields and, three hours later, we are getting close to the Himalayan mountains.

Across from me, sits a young woman wearing a nosering. She is dressed in a bright red sari and a blue headscarf and is wearing sandals. A boy and a girl are clinging to her, their eyes fixed on us in wonder, their expressions saying: 'Who are they, what do they want?' Although their faces are smeared from running noses, one can see the fine translucent skin underneath.

The bus rumbles monotonously through the scenery. Most of the travellers seem to be asleep. At the first pit stop, some exchange seats, some go outside to relieve themselves, and some seem sick from the swaying of the bus. The road we are on, close to Tibet near Kodari, and strategically important, was built by the Chinese, a present to the Communist party of Nepal.

At lunchtime, our Indian Tata stops in Barabise at some primitive wooden shacks. I suspect that the bus drivers draw a little commission from these places by supplying them regularly with tourists for meals. Gyaltsen orders nine portions of *dal bhat* and Carolin, who is our finance minister starting today, pays the bill. Although I am hungry, I shudder at the sight of the food. I decide to stick to the rice. The lentils and the few pieces of vegetables are cold. Even though I am familiar with the eating habits of the simple people in Asia, I have still to get used to watching them mash up the food with dirty fingers and shove it into their mouth by holding the plate right in front of it. They always eat with their right hand; the unclean left has to remain at their back or on the lap. I hope they cannot read the aversion on my face.

A group of poorly dressed children hanging around me, laughing, ask me, 'What's your name?' or 'Give me sweet.' Andi and Ebi take some shots with the film camera. Another five hours to Jiri. The bus makes frequent stops for the locals to get on and off. Our group are the only tourists on this bus. The road becomes increasingly winding and the bus slower. Andi looks green in the face and ill. The forest has now given way to terraced fields and the occasional hamlet. For the past hour the second driver has taken over while the first driver is sleeping. The two music cassettes are constantly repeated. We have now been listening to the same music for hours, as if we were being conditioned for our musical trek. This is a bit too much for my taste.

Eventually, the terrain becomes more level. Some of the travellers are getting restless, a sign that the twelve hour trip is nearing its end. The highway cuts through green rice fields and the first houses of Jiri appear. Another turn and the bus rolls into the parking lot. It is 5 p.m. Totally stiff and tired, we descend from the bus into a screaming crowd of young children. 'Have you a pen? — Give me sweet!'

Andi is on top of the bus to help with the unloading. His special attention is always directed to the double bass. The rest of our equipment, other than the precious accordion, is not really very fragile. But here we find out that our two solar lamps, which should have made us independent of electricity, are missing. Annoying, but there is nothing we can do about it now. Not only the children, but also our porters, are expecting us at the bus stop. Tsewang, Gyaltsen's son-in-law, is a Sherpa. The other four, Manpuri, Chiete, Harka and Asman, are Tamang's; all are very pleasant chaps, aged from eighteen to twenty-four. Chiete is the youngest and, perhaps for that reason, I take a liking to him. Before we get a chance to look around, the luggage is already on the shoulders of the Tamangs, with only the light backpacks left for us.

Jiri is a village built mostly along the road. Left and right, close together, are stately and very nice whitewashed houses with shingle roofs. Most of them have a balcony; window- and door frames are painted blue or brown. Attached to the outside walls are scaffold-like wooden structures, which serve to dry corncobs, pumpkins, hay and laundry. How simple and useful! No waste of energy, nor pollution. Jiri certainly is the main town or, more precisely, main village of the whole region. There is no other place with as many stores that offer food supplies, hardware, general goods or any other basic items, as this village at the end of the highway. In Jiri, situated at the access road to the Solo Khumbu, the Rai, Chhetri, Sherpa, Kumbar and Sunwar, live in peaceful coexistence. The latter work mostly as gold- and silversmiths.

Gyaltsen has chosen the Sange Lodge. He knows this Sherpa family, who rent up to fifteen beds to trekkers. On the way to the lodge at the western end of the village, we are accompanied by an army of curious locals. Children and young Sherpa women, whom we recognise by their colourful horizontally striped aprons, lead our peculiar and exotic trek in their long and heavy wool skirts, scarves wrapped around their waists and adorned with precious necklaces made of silver, coral, lapis lazuli and amber. Their long, black hair is usually artfully entwined, showing a pronounced parting. As I had already noticed on my previous visit to Nepal, the Sherpani women are often quite tall.

With bows and the ever-endearing *Namaste*, we are welcomed at the Sange Lodge. The entrance is fairly low and we have to back up with our bulky double bass, to manoeuvre it through. Without delay, the hostess shows us our quarters; it is clean but spartan. The toilet smells a bit strong. Gyaltsen asks us to a welcome tea hour: 'Tea time!' he always calls happily. We are crouching in the narrow kitchen, which is a fire pit surrounded by an arrangement of aluminium bowls and copper kettles on the walls. We are giggling like small children, happy that an idea, born in the far-away Wetterstein, has become reality.

We decide to play music later. But first we need a few *dokos*, the carrying baskets made of bamboo. Gyaltsen knows exactly what we need and picks five of them at a neighbour's, across the street. We also get some rope to secure things, and I plead for a few umbrellas, just in case. All our activities and business are conducted under the scrutiny of countless children who follow every movement with curious eyes and runny noses.

'Everything ready and clear now?' I ask around.

A young Sherpani holding her child.

'And what do we do with the generator?' Andi asks in his Allgäu dialect.

I had secretly hoped in Kathmandu that we would not have to haul this monster along.

'Gyaltsen, where do you think we will not have electricity?' I ask.

'I think, Nuntala, Bupsa and Surkhe, but from Surkhe we could walk to Lukla, where they have electricity, and load our batteries. So, really, only Nuntala and Bupsa are without electricity.'

'What do *you* think?' I address all.

'Leave it here!' a chorus responds.

'What about returning the thing to Kathmandu?' I ask and propose the following: 'If possible, I will make a phone call today to Klaus Wanger. Tsewang could take it back by bus and return immediately. Without baggage he can catch up with us. How do you feel about that?'

They all voice agreement or quietly nod their heads.

Darkness has fallen and the occasional street lantern gives the village a warm and cosy atmosphere, even by night. Sange Lodge is serving supper: potatoes and vegetables, milk tea or beer. After dinner, we unpack our instruments. My dulcimer has retained its tuning, thanks to the insulating pads. I provide the 'A' of my tuning fork for correct tuning. We are crammed into the kitchen, which is narrow, even without instruments or audience. Around us are faces reflecting curiosity and expectation. Gyaltsen will be our interpreter. He is sitting in a dark corner; his sparkling gold tooth signals his location. Erich looks at Carolin, Carolin at Beeker, Beeker at the guitarists Malte and Simon; the two look towards me. Bingo! The first piece is a catchy Salzburg tune in 2/4 time, with a few nice minor chords. I notice with relief that the Sherpas are beaming after a few chords. Gyaltsen explains that in Europe the audience applauds a performance they like by clapping their hands. Here, this is not the custom; it would take a special invitation to do so. Gyaltsen continues. I figure he is telling them about our musical evenings at the hut.

During the preparations for our journey, we had all agreed that we would only perform for the local Nepalese, not for tourists. We would have more fun and enjoyment playing music casually without pressure and formal engagements; this would give us more independence while travelling.

After a few Bavarian pieces, Gyaltsen announces *Resham Firiri* and two other Nepali songs. While they had already sounded wonderful on the balcony of the Shree Antu, they sound even more enchanting and at home here, in the intimate atmosphere of the Sherpa kitchen. Often melodies and folk songs like these originate in living rooms and kitchens. And while we are playing the third Nepali song, my thoughts wander back to the day when I met Gyaltsen.

Ang Gyaltsen Sherpa

The name Gyaltsen in the Sherpa language means Thursday. The first time I came across his name was in Peter Matthiessen's book *The Snow Leopard*. The expedition documented in the book, led by the biologist George Schaller, included Sherpa Tukten, Thu Tsering, Dawa, Sherpa Jangbu and a Sherpa called Gyaltsen. It went into the interior of the Dolpo, with the purpose of tracing and studying blue sheep and the extremely rare snow leopard. Matthiessen participated in this expedition as a journalist. This resulted in a book with remarkable insight, as well as suspense. I liked it a lot and the name Gyaltsen had stuck in my mind.

On 6 February 1993, a Saturday, I was flying from Kathmandu to Lukla on a small plane of Royal Nepal Airlines. On the same day, I continued to Chomoa, just outside the Sagarmatha National Park. The weather was brilliant and I felt privileged to have this impressive first view of the Himalayan peaks. In Chomoa I was rewarded with another highlight, when at night, the moon rose above the 6,000 metre high Thamserku. The next day, I climbed further in the direction of Namche Bazar. Only a few tourists were en route but all of those who came from the higher regions raved about the fantastic scenery and seemed extremely pleased.

On the steep climb below Namche Bazar, I was paying the price for not getting acclimatised. I had trouble breathing and suffered an excruciating headache. Exhausted, I finally reached the first houses of the village. At first glance, it was like being transposed into an amphitheatre. The houses were

Thamserku and Sange Ri.

built like steps into the slope and high above them rose the 6,000 metre mountains — Thamserku with its wild rugged peaks, and Sange Ri, with a white cap. I paused at the village stream for a while. Prayer flags were fluttering about a decorated *stupa*. This symbolic Buddhist structure stands for the All-embracing, with one half of a spherical stone under the soil, the other half above. A square, on top of it, has a pair of eyes on each side, thus looking in all directions. Design of the

Stupa in Namche Bazar.

world, universal model of the cosmos, symbol for life and stages toward revelation — all these possibilities of interpretation are inherent to a *stupa*.

There, by the white *stupa*, where the stream was harnessed

in white stone blocks, the washing and laundry place of Namche Bazar, was also the favourite meeting place for the young and old. I walked toward one of the oldest houses and stepped into the courtyard, where a woman, sitting in a yoga position, was keeping her husband and a little girl company.

Namaste, I greeted them and a friendly *Namaste* was the response. Like almost all the inhabitants of Namche Bazar, this family belonged to the Sherpa tribe. The head of the family, a friendly looking man — I guessed about fifty-year's old, was cleaning his sleeping bag; the woman was having tea. The little girl was chasing a ball.

The Sherpa asked: 'How are you?'

'I am fine.'

'What's your name?'

'I'm Charly.'

I liked the warmth in his voice and his confidence. He introduced me to Gyalmo, his wife and his grandchild. Soon we were deep in conversation and I mentioned my work at the mountain hut. Luckily, I had a postcard of the Reintalanger Hut with me, which I could show him. He was excited and asked me if I needed extra help for the summer. I was completely surprised by the question and was not sure if it was meant seriously. But I asked him for his address and explained that this was something that had to be planned ahead and that I could not promise anything now. He fully understood. But I already knew that I would love to have him. I just had to have the right circumstances.

In April of the same year, when I was just recovering from pneumonia, which I had contracted in Nepal, I received a tragic letter from Gyaltsen. His wife had suddenly died of an infection. If at all possible, he would like to come to Germany this summer. I was worried about him and sent him a plane ticket with the necessary application for a visitor's visa. For almost two months I did not hear anything from Gyaltsen, no phone call, no mail, no sign at all.

On 4 July the telephone rang: Sherpa Gyaltsen. With excitement in his voice, he told me that he would be arriving in Frankfurt the next day by Royal Nepal Air Lines. He caught me by surprise, but in record time I arranged for my brother Werner to pick him up at Frankfurt Airport. The following day, friends who were planning to come up to the hut, would bring him along to the Werdenfels country.

We had a nice reunion and Gyaltsen was happy because, the scenery of the Wetterstein was so similar to his home. In the weeks to come, we kept wondering about the serendipity, that had brought us together, and the coincidence that the short encounter in February would result in a close friendship. Bit by bit, he told me details of the sudden death of his wife, to whom he had been married for thirty-five years. I learnt that a traditional funeral of a Sherpa can be very costly and bring families to the edge of ruin. I tried to encourage him and slowly he gained confidence.

Slowly Gyaltsen told me his life story. At the age of fifteen he had worked as a porter, with the Hillary expedition in 1953, the first successful Everest climb. 'Then, we were 1,500 porters. We had to carry about 30 kg from Bhaktur to the Everest base camp. The money alone, which had to be paid to the porters later, required six of them, because Nepal at that time had only coins, no notes.' Later Gyaltsen participated in a Japanese, an Italian and an Indian Everest expedition. With every one of them, he had reached the South Ridge at 8,000 metres. Unfortunately, there had never been enough oxygen for him to climb to the summit. At that time, it had been very disappointing for him, but now he was reconciled.

At the age of twenty he had married the fifteen-year-old Gyalmo. They had had five children, but three of them had died shortly after birth. They were left with two girls. Serki, the younger, had now taken over the running of the parental household and Gyaltsen was by now the proud grandfather of five grandchildren. He is loving and kind but also firm. He loves children above all, and many a time, I see him interact affectionately with children at the hut.

For seven years now, he has belonged to our team at the Reintalanger Hut. With his friendly, but firm ways he has become essential for us. During the stress of the main season his sensitivity and understanding make him a balancing force. In particular, he enjoys social evenings with games, which break the daily routine of life at the hut. When guests ask for Sherpa Gyaltsen, he feels honoured. He has a healthy self-confidence. The right atmosphere is important to him, as the prayer flags and the prayer wheel at the Partnach demonstrate. He loves travelling the world, especially places in the mountains like Chamonix, Grindelwald or the Sexten Dolomites, but he is also interested in cities, like Venice, Munich, Frankfurt and Zurich. He likes to leaf through magazines and to listen to music. However, when he is looking at books on Nepal, during a lull, I see a touch of homesickness, a longing for his home, Namche Bazar. To keep himself from becoming too nostalgic, he usually hums or whistles a tune from his repertoire of Sherpa songs to himself.

Prayer wheel at the Partnach.

We are Short of a Porter

Here, in his mountains, Sherpa Gyaltsen is the undisputed chief. This has already become apparent over the last three days. This is quite in contrast to his attitude during the summer months at the Reintalanger Hut, where he keeps in the background. Now he makes the decisions, and we go along respectfully. For one thing, we know we are in good, experienced hands. He speaks the various dialects of the local people, takes the initiative in waking everyone up and looks after everyone's well-being during our trekking. Secondly, his acting as Sirdar or leader gives us a welcome sense of security and comfort.

Mercilessly, he knocks at our door at 5:45 a.m. 'Good morning! It's six thirty! Breakfast!' It is especially tough for our pathological late risers. The lodge's owners also have to get up early. Gyaltsen knows what he is doing. This morning, before we start the first stage of our trek to Shivalaya, all the luggage has to be distributed to the porters.

The evenings are as lively, as the morning hours are quiet. Only really necessary words are spoken: 'What do you like, Carolin, Tibetan bread or *chapatti*? And you?' The majority decides what we will eat. Most of the time it is Tibetan bread. It is amazing how it makes your stomach feel full. Butter is a luxury; however, there is plenty of honey and artificially coloured ruby red jam. With it, everyone gets two cups of milk tea, that's it for breakfast — a bit spartan.

Gyaltsen checks the bill and Carolin, our finance minister, pays it in the smoky Sherpa kitchen.

Gyaltsen's voice now takes on a sharpness which I do not associate with him. In Nepali he commands Harka, Manpuri, Chiete, Asman and Tsewang on the terrace. Dawn is just breaking and the first villagers are on their way, wrapped up for the cold. Gyaltsen energetically springs in to action and divides the luggage without pity, it seems, although he has been a porter himself. Poor Chiete! The youngest gets the most: Erich's accordion, Ebi's camera tripod, sleeping bags, clothes, and some of his own food ration. Harka and Manpuri do not fare much better: the guitars, the tenor horn, all 20 kg of my dulcimer, the first aid kit and their own food and clothes. Asman seems to have drawn the trump card with the double bass. Despite its size, it is fairly light but terribly bulky and awkward to carry. Tsewang is to return the generator by bus to Kathmandu. He will be missed by our Tamang porters, who do not utter a single complaint.

The Tamang are one of the largest groups of indigenous people in Nepal. They live mostly in the lower regions between 1,600 and 2,300 metres. Many of them are farmers, carpenters, or masons. The women weave winter coats and make bamboo baskets. In the past, the Tamang were horse traders. 'Ta' in Tibetan, means Horse, 'mang' is trader.

While Andi and Ebi are filming and I am busy taking pictures, we are again surrounded by a curious crowd of villagers. The sky is cloud-covered and it is relatively cool. Looking at our light backpacks, we sympathise with the Tamang, who are just picking up their load. Not to mention their shoes: one of them wears light cloth slippers, another one, sandals!

'Namaste', we say goodbye to the owners of Sange Lodge and march, single file, in a southeasterly direction away from Jiri, still accompanied by a group of villagers as far as the outskirts; then we are alone, at the foot of a healthy green, wooded slope. Very soon our line pulls apart: the camera people, the smokers, the mountain climbers, Gyaltsen, as the guide through his home turf, is at the head. Carolin and I are last and soon we notice that Ebi, cameraman No. 1 with back-pack, tripod and camera, is falling back. He is smoking and looks like Christ on the way of the cross. We are starting to worry about him. 'I wish we had the other porter here. In this condition Eberhard will not make it very far.'

As if a prayer had been heard, down below, out of the woods, comes a young man dressed in a worn grey suit, white woollen cap, and rubber boots. A thin moustache and neglected teeth do not diminish the effect of his friendly smile. Spontaneously, we ask if he has time and if he would care to help us with the luggage to Shivalaya. We would guarantee him payment and food. He wants to know where we are headed. We explain that Namche Bazar is our final destination. For a moment he seems suspicious, but then introduces himself as Pemba, a Sherpa, and says that for now he will join us for the day. Carolin and I can hardly believe our luck as Pemba takes over Ebi's backpack with a grin.

An hour later we reach a high plateau. The sky is now completely clear; the rhododendron forest has given way to an alpine pasture. At a *bhatti*, (tea room), we all meet again for a refreshment. There is a light wind. I remind my friends to take off their sweat-soaked clothes because a cold could really spoil the fun and hamper our progress. We leave Ratmate behind; Mali will be the next village. Repeatedly, we pass farms with modest buildings and similar scenery. In front of them, neatly dressed women are sorting grain, corn is hung below the house gables for drying, children are playing in the yards, a cocky rooster is crowing, chicken are scratching for worms.

At the end of the plateau, at the point of descent, there is a group of big rocks strewn about, as if inviting us to rest for a while. We take in the scenery: two pristine ice peaks rise high above a ridge of wooded mountains in the distance to the northwest. The one to the left is the 7,000 metre high Numbur. Mountains as prominent as this, are often revered as sacred by local people. We are all impressed by this fantastic

On the road to Shivalaya.

view of terraced fields, gentle hills and the peaks of the Solo
Khumbu, especially our Himalayan novices. We regret that we
cannot stay longer at this enchanting vantage point.

Serpentines lead us down into the valley of the Khimti
Khola river. We rest once more in the vicinity of the village
Dovan. We enjoy hot noodle soup and milk tea at a *bhatti*.
This will have to do until we get to Shivalaya. A relatively
new-looking suspension bridge, made of steel ropes and steel
bars, constructed by a Swiss company, takes us across the river
into the fertile valley. Two men with prehistoric tools are

Arrival at Shivalaya.

working a felled tree, slowly and patiently trying to slice it into boards. When I request their permission to take a picture of them, they simply nod and stay concentrated on their job.

A little further on, the first houses of Shivalaya appear to the right. To our left stretches a narrow pine forest. There are still a few alder, oak and walnut trees. Here and there a butterfly flutters by. For a while we can hear various song birds, then their voices are drowned out by the roaring of the river below. Shivalaya is a dreamy, picturesque village, which could not be situated more idyllically. Protected by gently sloping hills, small stone houses are strung along the mountain river, painted brown, beige or blue. Gyaltsen has rushed ahead to organise our quarters and to negotiate a good price. Food and tea are already ordered.

The lodges are all quite similar: the beds are custom-made of wood, the kitchen has a stone stove. Kerosene stoves are not common yet. Considering the advance of deforestation, we would like to see more of them. We realise that tourists like us are partly the cause of this development. Already before our arrival, word has spread that a music group is on the way from Jiri to Namche Bazar. Our 'big guitar' in its black case alone, has probably provided enough evidence for the spreading of such news. Asman Tamang has carried it here without a problem. Now the porters are sitting on the ground of the village square, behind them are the villagers; women in red skirts, green sweaters and colourful clothes, men adorned with khukris, the Nepalese curved daggers. Curious brown faces are watching from windows, grubby children are standing on benches; in the middle of all this is our music group from Bavaria and Baden-Wüttemberg. It is still light and the temperature is pleasant. We decide to unpack the instruments and perform a little concert. Malte and Simon are tuning the guitars; one leg on the bench, Beeker has arranged his small percussion behind us. Beeker, landscape gardener in Stuttgart, has been playing with Carolin and Erich for quite some time. Although he is more of a solo traveller, who has already seen a bit of the world, he fits so well into our group of individualists, that I would not want to miss his easy, boyish manner and warm character.

The sound of the instruments fills the village square and we notice how trusting, friendly, and amazed eyes look at us while we are playing. This was our intention, to see happy native people, for whom we would gladly play *Resham Firiri* a second and third time.

A young child from the village.

The Tamang

Ulrich Gruber

Leaving the Siwalik mountains behind us, crossing the Mahabharat mountain range into the central mountain region of Nepal, one encounters peoples of Tibeto-Mongolian origin. They are divided into several smaller and larger tribes who, despite their common central Asian origin, often substantially differ in customs, traditions and language. The most numerous of these tribes are the Tamang. Their settlement covers mainly the region of the Kathmandu valley, in the East, reaching beyond the Su Koshi valley, and in the West, to the Buri Gandaki valley. Often, they have pronounced Tibetan facial features, although the origin of their ancestors' occupation of the southern side of the Himalayas, goes back a long way. There is a nice legend, telling the story of the immigration of the Tamang into this region: 'Long, long ago there lived a white cow beyond the high snow-covered mountains. This cow had three sons, Thenggu, Lunggu and Tulgu. One day, when the three brothers were standing in the pasture, a forceful gust took Tulgu far across the icy mountains to the south slopes of the Ganesh Himal. There he was married to a human girl, and his offspring were the Tamang. Over the years they spread through the many neighbouring valleys, the area they occupy today.'

The Tamang are alpine farmers with a strong sense of independence, but devoted to all those they consider friends. They speak their own Tibeto-Burmese language, but do not have their own script. The men wear a traditional jacket made of milled wool, with short sleeves and fringes at the back. Not only does it look smart, but it is also practical during monsoon rains. It is water repellent because the natural grease is not removed from the wool. All Tamang men wear a white scarf wrapped around their waist, which holds the traditional curved, all-purpose dagger. The houses of the Tamang are built solidly, usually two storeys high with a porch as extended living space, constructed of wood shingles and stone tiles. The lower level is for cooking, eating, sleeping and living. The upper storey contains the harvest and staples, as well as tools. There are particularly stately Tamang houses, with tiled courtyards and masterfully carved window frames, in the Dhunche area, at the upper Trisuli river. In these, the living area is upstairs while the lower floor has the stables and pantries.

The Tamang are Buddhists and wear the red cap of the orthodox Nyingmapa sect of Tibetan Buddhism. Their villages have a modest Gompa, (cloister), in the style of farmhouses. The interior contains temple rooms for the Lamas' recitations and tantric rituals. The Tamang communicate their spiritual relations to the realm of magic powers and demons, not only through these priests, but also through the *djakri*, (shaman).

The community of the Tamang is divided into family clans which rule over marriages. So it is possible that members of the same clan cannot marry, while other clans may allow it. Marriage, divorce and extramarital relationships are treated casually, in a way a sign of the secure and confident, relatively free, status of women in Tamang society. Women rule the family and household. They do not hesitate to state their opinions vigorously to their men folk. Tourism of the modern era has provided an additional income for many Tamang men, in their role as porters. Tamang's are excellent carriers of heavy loads, and are strong and reliable. They are preferably used on trekking and climbing expeditions; sometimes they are promoted to personal companion, cook or even Sirdar. During my treks in the Nepalese mountains, I have always enjoyed the company of Tamang's, who have always proved to be reliable, with a wonderful sense of humour and a particular love of singing. Unforgettable are two Tamang porters on a trek to the foot of the 8,000 metre high Makalu. A traveller had become sick and was unable to walk. For three days they carried him in a bamboo basket down into the valley. Taking turns, they hauled the heavy load over the most difficult terrain for long hours. In the end there was no one as relieved and happy as the two Tamangs when the patient finally recovered at a lower altitude, so attached had they become to the man for whom they felt responsible.

In recent years, the Tamang have developed more confidence. They do not want to be seen any longer as backward mountain farmers but want to prove that they are part of the economical and social progress, based on their own resources and initiatives. With the foundation of a relief fund, whose president is a Tamang, they have created an organisation which promotes developing projects for villages and contributes to better living conditions for poor villagers.

Summer Time

Shivalaya still lies in the shade as we are leaving. At the village square, we recognise several people who were present at our musical offering last night. There is also the little girl in the blue dress, whom I had been watching for a while, playing with a little ball attached to a length of elastic. She seemed to have invented her own version of the yo-yo. Laughingly, they demand *Resham Firiri*, but our instruments are already packed and the Tamang are just about to pick up their load. We let them go ahead. Today's climb will be more than 1,000 metres — not a stroll. After Carolin has paid the hostess, we are ready to leave, too. *'Namaste — Namaste'*. With smiles on their faces, the villagers wave goodbye, as we leave Shivalaya, one after the other. We pass women, who are spreading grain to dry in braided baskets. On the other side of the village, two men are carrying driftwood up from the riverbank.

With my finger guiding me through my Nepali phrase book, I read, stumblingly, to Gyaltsen: *'Yo Bhatto Bhandarma dsane kati ghanta lagcha?* (How far is it from here to Bhandar?')

Gyaltsen answers with a warm smile: *'Chhar paanch kosh ghanta'* (Four to five hours), and, grinning from ear to ear, he adds: *'Bis taare jaane'* (We will walk slowly). *'Mero pachhi aaunos'* (Follow me).

My friends, observing our conversation, burst out laughing. Well — one has to start somewhere!

Outside Shivalaya the path starts to climb. Relatively dry, it leads through pine and rhododendron, interspersed with fern, bamboo, and various greens unknown to me. Past the woods, the terraced fields start.

In Sangbadanda, a tiny hamlet, we have some tea. The breaks for refreshments serve two purposes. Obviously, we have to take in enough water, but it is also the perfect way to keep contact on the road. Of course, it is a chance to have a cigarette too and a few encouraging words. Being together on the road really gives us an insight into our social being.

Here and there, we notice a poorly maintained hut. Usually there are cackling chickens about; a dog barks at us, we hear some birds, then a transistor radio blaring in a courtyard, or the song of one of the porters, with the typical Nepalese rhythm. There are so many impressions, on various levels, that some details elude us, I am sure. I am reflecting on this simple life in the country and how little one really needs. Here, there is just one well for water, no electricity, definitely no telephone, occasionally a radio, but the people seem to be happy. This might change within ten years. When imagining the joys of the simple life, we should not forget that these people live in poverty day-in and day-out. Would we really want this? It may be easy to drop out for a short time, exist on a financial minimum, when we always have the security of having a bank account. Nevertheless, the memory of this is very important, to make us realise how privileged we are, if only to make us *feel* privileged.

Most of the time, it is the prayer flags and mani walls that announce a hamlet. There are no such things here as signs with place names. The name of a village can sometimes be found on an advertising board like 'Sangbadanda Lodge. Hot Shower.' When we feel lost, Gyaltsen is there to save us. *'Chiya aune manparcha'*, (We will have tea). To pause at the right time and to drink as much liquid as possible, more than normal, is quite important when trekking, at least as important as changing into dry clothes.

Our porters, with their heavy loads, need the breaks even

more than we do. I dig out a pack of Camels from my back-pack and hand it to Asman. He shares the cigarettes with the other porters.

We are travelling off-season and enjoy the fact that there are so few tourists. Today, though, we have not one but two big surprises. First there is a young woman coming towards us. As it turns out, she is from Peiting in Upper Bavaria. Then a man approaches, about thirty, who looks familiar. He has stayed at the Reintalanger Hut a few times. Sometimes the world seems like a village.

During our tea time, a group of local people has gathered around us again, two women with artfully braided hair, both in Burgundy red clothes, with shiny nose- and earrings, and five happy, energetic children with dishevelled hair. As we are talking to each other, they repeat everything after us, waiting for the next word. In between we hear the familiar 'What's your name?' or 'Have you sweets?' We would love to talk more to them but have to press on for Bhandar. Lunch will be in Deorali, close to the first of the higher passes.

'What's for lunch?' Carolin asks.

'*Thukpa*, of course!' Beeker is quick to answer in his Swabian dialect.

'And tonight?' Erich asks with a big grin.

'*Dal bhat!* Delicious *dal bhat*.' Ebi throws in.

Our daily meals are almost identical. Who would not prefer a little more variety? But it is difficult to cook something interesting for a big group. It would take too much time. The way these funny, sometimes ironical or teasing remarks about unimportant things fly back and forth, tell me that the group is interacting well and enjoying our adventure. All is well!

Sometimes we pass a single house with a primitive stable next to it, which is barely covered with a roof of braided straw. In the shade of one of these stands a water buffalo with a calf. Annoyed, she tosses her head, with long curved horns, back and stares at me, with impenetrable black eyes as if to ask,

'What are *you* doing here?' At another farm there is a well. Girls, singing, are filling pitchers; two women are washing laundry in aluminium bowls and an old man with a furrowed face is brushing shoes. Close by stands a tin vase, as if it were just placed there for a still life. A little further along, women are cooking rice over a fire pit. The sun is breaking through the cloudy sky and brightens up the otherwise brown and dull landscape.

Occasionally, along the roadside, we encounter the typical resting walls, carefully put together, layer by layer, by the local people. They have two levels, one to sit on and a higher one as a backrest and to rest the backpack on. But this is only a secondary use. Foremost, they are monuments for the deceased, and they often have built in memorabilia, Gyaltsen explains to us. Our porters have their own walking rhythm and they pause more often, to set their *dokos* on the stone walls. Since I am the person bringing up the rear, I often catch up with them, after following the swinging neck of the double bass case, which rises above everything else and, to my amusement, is sometimes all I can see in front of me. It is almost the exact image I had visualised months ago, while thinking about our trek.

Soon we will be in Deorali. We are passing a few houses. On the front step of one of these, a young woman sits with a baby and crochets. There are a few brown wooden bowls standing on the wall, with onions, garlic and vegetables. Corncobs are hanging in the drying structures. A tiny general store has opened its shutters and, in passing, I can smell soap. I have fallen back. There is no one in sight. Finally, I too, reach the little village on this high plain, about 2,700 metres high. Gyaltsen has already ordered the obligatory noodle soup. The chilli here in Deorali tastes much hotter and my mouth is aflame. Our peaceful and quiet meal is only interrupted by the occasional coughing attack, due to the spices, and our laughter. Gyaltsen pours milk tea for relief. A herd of donkeys trots by, their bells breaking the silence of our lunch in an idyllic way. Two young women, in canvas slippers, are walking by in small, delicate steps, as if dancing, despite their heavy load. Everything here is carried on one's back, with the help of a support belt of braided hemp, held by the forehead. Men with particularly heavy loads, would carry the so-called *dogma*, a traditional support stick on which they can rest the basket, while taking a short break, without having to set it on the ground.

We decide to skip the planned midday concert for Deorali because our Tamang porters are cooking their own lunch somewhere, and that is where our instruments are. Leaving the little romantic village, we descend slowly. Bhandar lies roughly 2,000 metres high. We pause again at a place where a whole family is working on the construction of a small house. Everyone, from small child to grandfather, is carrying heavy stones on cradles. With hammer and chisel, they split giant rocks, which will become their home thirty metres above. In view of these heavy stones, our backpacks seem much lighter now. Slightly embarrassed, I take a few photos.

Brought up to help at an early age.

Two young girls on the road.

Dark green forests alternate with light clearings. On the opposite side of the valley, we can see a few white houses gleaming in the sunlight. Higher mountains are reaching for the sky on the horizon. Through the haze, we can see our destination for tomorrow, Sete. For now, we are still headed for Bhandar. The path is getting increasingly steep toward the Likhu Khola valley and then widens into a road, which is lined by cornfields and hedges.

Knowing that we have almost reached our destination, I am in no hurry to get there. Instead, I am falling way behind, trotting along slowly, all by myself, happily enjoying the afternoon sun, nodding and smiling at people passing by and villagers sitting in front of their houses. Then, two *stupas*, glowing in the sun, come into sight. Passing an apple orchard and strings of prayer flags, I finally arrive at the Buddha Lodge, beside the *stupas*, at the western entrance of the village, where the road widens into a lovely picturesque courtyard. The Tibetan prayer flags look very colourful against the blue sky. They are printed with the Buddhist prayer, *Om mani padme hum* (Hail to the Jewel in the Lotus). The colours, white, blue, red, yellow, and green, together symbolise the earth and the universe. Wherever these flags wave weightlessly in the air, they lend a certain tranquillity and lightness to their location.

The sun has already disappeared behind the hills, when we finally unpack our instruments. It is cooling down quickly. The instruments are slightly out of tune. We have a very small audience for our late afternoon concert as we are at the outskirts of the village. It makes for a nice atmosphere, though. There is complete silence; a light wind softly moves the branches of the apple trees. So we play soft pieces: *Mountain Melody*, a minuet and *Life Story*, both very slow and melancholic. During the intermission, we get into our down jackets. We are shivering. To warm up, we play two faster pieces: the *Bavarian Tailor* and *Counter Dance*, then the Nepalese songs. Gyaltsen does not need to do a lot of explaining, since we are playing mostly for ourselves. The hostess of the Buddha Lodge, our quarters for the night, is standing in the door with her family and, just in time for *Resham Firiri*, a group of villagers arrives. Today it is *Nepali 2*, with its soft minor chords, that seems to be in tune with the prayer flags, the *stupas*, and the beginning of dusk. While the gold-red evening sky above the mountains heralds the night, we all sink into complete tranquillity and contentment. As if to deepen our contemplative state, Carolin quietly tunes into a melancholic double bass solo of *Summer Time*, the highlight of the day.

Carolin

I met Carolin, in the summer of 1991, at the Reintalanger Hut. The employees of the Alternative pub, Casino, in Stuttgart had chosen this destination for their company outing. Strange coincidence, or was it?

Weeks before, Tommi and Josie, had been entrusted with the task of finding a nice mountain hut, in a beautiful location with atmosphere. One warm, early summer day, the two came sliding down the eastern slopes of the snowfields of the *Zugspitze*-plateau, or what was left of it. They were fascinated by the view into the Reintal and the mountain range, from the peaks of the solitary *Platt* peak and the rugged *Gatterl* peaks, to the striking shapes of the *Hoher Kamm*. To the left was the 1,200 metre wall of the *Kleiner Wanner*, next to it, the higher ridges of the *Hochwanner*, and behind that, the proud guardians of the Reintal: the *Höhlenkopf* and the *Jungfernkarkopf*.

After quenching their thirst at the *Knorr Hut*, they arrived on the terrace of the Reintalanger Hut. It was then that Tommi and Josie knew this was the right place for their purpose. Back in Stuttgart, they gave it a rave review. Not long after that, I received a request to reserve fifteen places for four days in August. I remember those days well. It seemed to me that Carolin was the head of the team. Among the whole group of Alternatives, with their outrageous hair colours, from peroxide blond to green streaks, she stood out; if not by colour, then by the bright colours of her clothes. She appeared to be the voice of the group, not by commanding but by her subtle firmness and ability to keep the group together.

In the evenings I usually sat with Markus Opitz and Tommi, with my dulcimer and the two guitars. The people at the Casino listened attentively, without speaking, or in other ways disrupting, as is so often the case.

Carolin liked the Bavarian folk music. The following year, they repeated their outing to the hut. I had been thinking about Carolin as my assistant, and just as I was about to ask her if she would like to take a summer job at the hut, she began her music study for the double bass. But in July 1995, it finally worked out. Carolin came to work for a month, as well as Peppi and Susanne. Gyaltsen Sherpa was visiting at the same time. Right from the start, everything ran very smoothly and it turned out to be my best team so far.

When I took over the lease of the Reintalanger Hut in 1986, I already owned a few instruments, among them a double bass, which I had acquired for the bargain price of 700 marks, ten years earlier. Built of maple and spruce in 1952 by a Mittenwald craftsman, this beautiful instrument had a particularly warm sound. Carolin practised on it every day, in order to keep in shape. The tough part of it was that Susanne had to join in with the guitar, and I with the dulcimer. That was the end of my afternoon naps. However, we enjoyed it enormously. Besides our traditional wake-up tune, we played, occasionally, either on the terrace, if the weather was nice, or in the evenings, in the dining room, after all the work was done. Often we played for a birthday or farewell of favourite guests. At that time Erich, Carolin's partner, visited more frequently. Soon, he was in charge of 'musical education and advancement' at the Reintalanger Hut.

The Casino fell victim to a legal battle later on, and the Schlesinger pub replaced it, at the same location. Carolin began playing professionally around that time; she is now involved with several music groups in Stuttgart. But every year, Carolin reserves time in July or August for the hut, as my right hand. Her good temper and radiant personality, and her unmistakable style of playing, whether it is classical music, Bavarian, jazz or reggae, make her popular with friends as well as her bands.

Surprise in Sete

At breakfast, I notice that Beeker, our percussionist, does not utter a word. He is wrapped up as if he were feeling very cold.

'Are you sick, Beeker?' I ask him.

'Oh, just a little cold.'

'Take care of yourself. You have to change those wet shirts as often as you can. Tomorrow we are going to cross a 3,500 metre pass.'

'I think I will be fine.'

Our Tamang carriers are already on the way, as we are waiting for Ebi at the *stupa*. He is the last one, almost every day. Gyaltsen does not like it if we get on the road with too much delay.

'Today we will have a nice landscape, but we need seven or eight hours to get to Sete. The path from Kenja to Sete, is very, very steep. Let's go!'

There is a little concern in his voice this morning. Aiming toward the river Likhu Khola, we leave Bhandar, the enchanting place of the white *stupas*, where a few chords of Carolin's bass solo are still floating about the prayer flags.

Below Bhandar, we sink into a stretch of deep green alder forest. This is extremely fertile ground. Numerous little creeks are bubbling downward in an eastern direction, towards the Likhu Khola; they are all tiny tributaries of the Holy River Ganges, Gyaltsen explains. After a while, our group stretches out again. Each morning Gyaltsen reminds us: 'Never walk faster than the porters; it would not be good for their morale.' Past the forest, the terrain starts dropping off toward the valley.

Gholunda is the next village. In the lower regions, close to the river, there are mostly Chhetri, Rai and Brahmin, living peacefully together. The village is enclosed by lush green terraced fields, alder, papaya and banana plants. All of these grow plentifully here. We even detect a few orange trees, loaded with fruit. A Brahmin family is sitting on a bench alongside their house, the grandparents, in their brown-red clothes, laughing; two little girls and their mother are dressed in the same colours. They are wearing strings of red glass beads and a braided wool scarf around their shoulders. The houses here are covered with shingles, and again, there are structures for drying hay and vegetables. Most of the houses have an ochre finish, overhangs are green-brown, windows and doorframes rather weathered. There are two or three tiny general stores, as well as a few *bhattis*. A jay shrieks from a papaya tree. A young Rai is climbing up the riverbed with a string of fish, to be hung up to dry in front of his house.

From the sun-drenched far side of the river, my eyes turn to the small farm that I am just passing. A few water buffaloes are grazing in the yard. A herd of mules is trotting up the serpentines, their bells ringing cheerfully. Wherever I look, charming scenarios seem to be competing with each other; here a flock of chickens scratching for worms, there a bunch of goats chewing leaves from the lower branches of an alder tree. Tidy stone walls frame the path on both sides. Beyond that, women are sorting potatoes; laughingly, they tell me in English, 'No good potatoes, very small.'

All morning I feel in harmony with nature, completely detached from everything else; free!

As I am stepping down the winding path towards the valley in a dreamlike state, I hear a whistle behind me. At first, I can't believe my eyes, but it is indeed Tsewang, finally catching up with us, after taking the rejected generator back to

A young Nepali mother.

Kathmandu. We are happy that he managed his task in record time. At the Greenwich hotel he had met Klaus Wanger, who not only took the generator back, but also gave him two presents for us. One, a bottle of whisky, he hands me right there and then. The other one is supposed to be a surprise for the evening in Sete.

We have reached the right bank of the Likhu Khola, hiking upstream. It is lined by elder trees, mixed with huge boulders, which we have to negotiate. We pass a long string of yellow flowers, spanning the river. Gyaltsen tells me that this is a sacred place for Hindus, where they come for prayers. I can see why. In retrospect, this is one of the most striking places on the trek between Jiri and Namche Bazar.

Spread over the meadows, are haystacks, and black-grey cattle grazing. Occasionally, we pass groups of porters, and Gyaltsen asks, *'Khan dsante ho?'* (Where are you going?). 'Namche Bazar,' they answer, usually without looking up. Underneath the huge heavy loads, mostly sacks of rice and other goods for the weekend market, they can hardly lift their heads without risking losing their balance. At one point I brush one of the loads in passing, and the porter stumbles and falls. I am angry at myself. 'How can you be so stupid!?' While helping him to get up and put his load back on, I realise how much they really carry. Gyaltsen, Tsewang and Ebi, who are close by, come to help lift the enormous weight. He is carrying over 200 pounds of oil cans to Namche Bazar. I am not surprised to hear that sometimes porters collapse and die under these loads.

Through a narrow winding belt of alder trees, we reach a group of single clay houses, where our friends are waiting. Finally, teatime! Including Tsewang, now our sixth porter, they are visibly relishing their Camel cigarettes. *'Ramro!'* (Good). So does Erich — always in his black-and-white Norwegian sweater, heavy woollen slacks and a toque — and Carolin, Ebi, Beeker and Simon, the second youngest. The few non-smokers are teasing the addicts. Near our rest stop, a farmer is checking the quality of his millet, by running it through his fingers on to a mat. His grubby-looking children are standing beside him. 'Sweet, sweet!' they beg with squeaky thin voices. 'Very poor people,' Gyaltsen remarks. For us, Europeans, impressions like these are unforgettable. Although we have seen many similar children in Kathmandu, here, so close, they have a greater impact on us. I find a bag of trail mix in my backpack and pour the contents into the held-out hands of the children.

Across an impressive blue suspension bridge, we reach the other side of the river and, shortly after that, Kenja. Not far from there, the Kenja Khola flows into the Likhu Khola. Kenja is a larger settlement and seems to be wealthier than the others we have passed. The reason for this is the strategic location of this village; it is at an important crossroad. Trekking paths and supply roads from all directions meet here. At a checkpoint, police verify our passports and trekking permits.

Andi, as usual, is ahead of the group, in order to preserve some particularly picturesque scenery and situations of the trek on film.

Kenja is populated mostly by Sherpas. Gyaltsen knows a family where we can eat. Only the women are home. *'Menyu kahaan chha?'*, (What's on the menu?), he asks. Instead of the daily noodle soup, we order potatoes with vegetables, which proves to be a mistake. Had we known that the vegetables still had to be picked from the garden, we would have stuck with the good old noodle soup. We have to wait over an hour. Gyaltsen is quite irritated and says he will not return here, especially since he thinks the food is overpriced. Despite this, we enjoy sitting here at the centre of Kenja, relaxing, watching the hustle and bustle and the *dzos* (a cross between yak and cattle) going by. The single porters always have a friendly *Namaste* for us. Finally: *'Linos!'* (Help yourself, bon appetit!) *'Mitho'*, (delicious), we answer Gyaltsen, rubbing our stomachs, as we finally enjoy our lunch in the smoky but warm Sherpa kitchen.

It is almost two o'clock when we shoulder our backpacks to continue. The Tamangs are already on the steep serpentines ahead. Asman and Harka are just disappearing around a bend, with double bass and dulcimer. Just watching them, I am so happy that I am not carrying their load. We have to climb another 1,000 metres to Sete. In the courtyard of a *bhatti*, with a fantastic view, we catch up with each other, all terribly thirsty. Against his usual habit, Erich has a Coke, while everyone else chooses hot lemon. On the next leg, we alternate the lead with two French women. We easily pass a porter, which is no big deal, considering he is hauling 70 kg of kerosene. From a clearing, we can see in the east the mountain range, which we will cross tomorrow. Below are a few white houses, Sete. Another two hours.

The sun has dropped behind the mountains of Bhandar and it is getting uncomfortably cold. I immediately switch my wet, light sweater for a dry but heavy one. Although we are all tired from the long hike today, we are in good spirits. We passed such beautiful landscapes.

We still meet porters with heavy loads and pitiful footwear; even late in the day, they greet us with a friendly *'Namaste'*, although they might not feel like it at all.

Gyaltsen stops at a stone rest just before 5 p.m. Andi is close by, filming. There is silence around us and the first stars are twinkling. No one says a word. We just enjoy the solemn atmosphere.

'Hami jo hotelma basne saktsaong?' (Can we stay for the night?) Gyaltsen breaks the silence to ask the owner of the next lodging. Dinner is served quickly because we have noodles. Wrapped in our down jackets we sit, closely huddled, in the small kitchen, very happy, enjoying our soup. Milk tea, hot lemon and a few bottles of beer do their bit. A Petromax burner provides light, yak dung the heat. But it does not get really warm, because the wind is whistling through the cracks.

The Sherpa family, with a few very alert and lively children, is already eagerly awaiting our music. Today I have to do some tuning on my dulcimer. The double bass is unpacked, as well as the accordion, guitars and tenor horn. Beeker is ready behind his percussion instruments, with slightly glassy eyes and reddish nose from his cold. Just as we are ready, Tsewang hands me a parcel. 'Surprise', he laughs. Everyone urges me to open it and two bottles of red wine appear, along with a letter from Klaus and Agathe. The letter contains another surprise. A friend of Klaus' had read a story, 'Bavarian Evening in a Mount Everest Hut', in the 7 December 1998 edition of the *Münchner Abendzeitung* (*Munich Evening Paper*), in which all our names are mentioned and, another surprise, spelt correctly. He had faxed it to Kathmandu on the same day, coincidentally when Tsewang came to deliver the machine. We are thrilled about the way things turned out, fax and all, delivered on 11 December at 6 p.m., into the centre of the Himalayas. Amazing!

When we eventually start playing, we are all a bit hyped up, but every single piece comes off smoothly and perfectly. Between numbers, we have a sip of red wine and Gyaltsen does his informative part. We have to play *Resham Firiri* not only a second, but a third time also, and we manage to play *Nepali 1* and *Nepali 2* without a single mistake. Today is one of those rare evenings where everything goes well. The Sherpas, seeing how content and infinitely happy we are tonight, are also happy.

Snow on the Lamjura Bhanjyang

Although low hanging clouds greet us the next day, we are all in the best of spirits. The fact that our trek, up to now, has been so harmonious, particularly last night, which was something of a highlight, gives us quite a boost. We are not the only ones to feel that way. The spark has sprung over to the porters, who are affected by our good mood.

As on previous days, we leave the lodge shortly after seven o'clock in the morning. A few dogs are barking nearby as we start filing into the rhododendron forest. The dusty path starts out quite steeply. 'Today we will cross the highest point of this trek, 3,500 metres,' Gyaltsen tells us. Now we know what to expect.

It is windy and cold. While last night the view of the hills of Bhandar was still clear, everything is now in a haze. The few porters whom we do meet disappear again instantly below the rhododendron cover. Gyaltsen looks up to the sky.

'*Adja thulo badal chha, hiu*' (Today big snow), he says to me. I worry about Beeker, whose cold has worsened. The prospect of a wet, cold day, for the long hike to Junbesi does not have a cheering effect on Beeker. Completely alone, he trots along. We only see him briefly at the first stop for a drink at a *bhatti*. Andi too, the strongest and best trained, is suffering. He has an attack of stomach flu and is almost constantly looking out for suitable bushes behind which to relieve his discomfort. Still, he is always ahead of the group, to find good shots for his film camera, for wide-angle shots of the group or the perfect foreground. Malte moves mostly at the end, trying to catch up after some meticulous picture taking. Simon is also ahead with his steady rhythm. Carolin and Erich form the connecting middle.

Suddenly the sun breaks through the clouds and the dark green roof of the gigantic rhododendrons, through which we struggle upward. Herbert Tichy wrote in one of his books on Nepal, 'Nepal in the fifties was a big enchanted garden of rhododendrons. With mass tourism, the ecological situation has constantly deteriorated.' There are protected areas in Nepal where it is forbidden to cut wood for any reason whatsoever. But even in those areas one can occasionally hear suspect noises coming from the forest. For local people, wood is still cheaper than kerosene. If they want kerosene, it has to be carried from Jiri to Namche Bazar or even further. We meet a few of those porters today.

After a stretch without any farms or *bhattis*, we pass a few hamlets and old moss-covered stone walls. Stone prayer tables are leaning against the wall, always carved with the same mantra: *Om mani padme hum.*

Our first tea break is in the Numbur Lodge. Two Sherpa women, in dark dresses with typical colourful striped aprons, holding children in their arms, are standing in a door frame, which must have been whitewashed at some time but has almost returned to its original state. 'Sweet, sweet!' we hear again. Gyaltsen always stays neutral, because giving candy to children is discouraged. But, what can you do when they look at you with their irresistible smiles? In one of my pockets I find some chewing gum, instead of candy.

Hot lemon and ginger tea have become our favourites, like the noodle soup for lunch. I hang up my soaked undershirt near the fire, to dry. To my horror, this expensive 'active underwear' shrinks as it dries; not exactly the 'active' I had in mind when I bought it. One of the smaller Tamang porters happily accepts it, as I hold it up for grabs. Andi's stomach is still rebellious. I 'prescribe' another portion of a Swedish herbal mix, hoping it will calm his stomach.

To get to Lamjura, below the pass of the same name, we need about an hour. Up here, where we start out, one stone wall follows another. Below the crest of the Lamjura Bhanjyang, on the west side, only a few single trees and brush grow. Boulders and scree now dominate the landscape. The terrain has become alpine. Cloud cover closes in again. A dense, dark grey wall of fog wraps the whole scenery into a mystical shroud. Suddenly, a herd of mules, without loads, break out of the fog with a loud ting-a-ling. They will pick up new goods in Jiri, destined for Junbesi. We only see the herdsman for a few seconds, then the whole apparition dissolves into the mist. For a while we can still hear the 'ha – ho, ha – ho.'

Suddenly, like a Fata Morgana, the Himalayan Buddhist Lodge towers in front of us in the thick fog. Tsewang is already inside to order our lunch, while Gyaltsen is patiently waiting outside the lodge until the last one of us, today Ebi, arrives. *'Khaana.* Food. Today, noodle soup with egg!' He announces this with his never tiring charm and an infectious giggle that makes us all break out into loud laughter. Our Tamangs have found a protected corner outside to cook their lunch in. Only Pemba, the Sherpa, eats with us. It looks to me as if, in the eyes of the Sherpas, the Tamangs are at least one step below them in the local hierarchy. Unless it is Gyaltsen's age that makes him act like a patriarch with the Tamang's.

Entering the interior of the lodge, we are blinded by the opulence of the furnishings. For the first time we realise that there are also wealthy people among the Sherpas. Furniture, carpets, hardware; everything appears to be of a high quality. We sit down on benches covered with small rugs, and are soon enjoying steaming hot tea. I contemplate how wonderful it would sound to play music in this room. But we cannot afford the time, and we don't want to impose on the porters to unpack and pack the instruments. Looking through the kitchen window, we are surprised at the heavy snow squall. It's a good thing that we bought two plastic sheets in Jiri. They are big enough to protect our instruments from snow or rain. Luckily, it stops soon; nevertheless, it looks dark enough to suspect there will be more of it. Therefore, although it is very cosy inside, we shorten our lunch break to get back on the road. Outside, a young woman with a backpack is bundling up her baby. Two big, black eyes look curiously at the dancing snowflakes.

We continue our walk upward past stone walls and prayer tables, to the crest of the Lamjura Bhanjyang pass. The snow is now falling so heavily that we can barely see a hundred metres. In addition to that, an extremely strong wind hits the top of the pass and we get into all our available warm clothes quickly. We don't need any more sick people. Although we cannot see the actual crest of the pass, we recognise it as a 'place of energy'. In some prominent locations, like the Sway-ambhunath temple in Kathmandu, certain mountain peaks,

Snow shower at Lamjura Bhanjyang Pass.

Night sky over Swayambhunath temple.

village squares, or in this case, the 3,550 metre high Lamjura pass, there are prayer flags. Attached to strings between several bamboo poles, which are stuck in the ground, are hundreds of these, many torn to pieces. Their loud flapping in the strong wind carries quite a distance. The entire scene of the flags in the mist and swirling snow, has something transcendental, metaphysical, even sacred about it. It becomes almost surreal when, out of the ever-increasing snow squalls, an elderly woman emerges, barefoot, in a heavy brown dress. She is holding on to a seemingly useless umbrella with holes, and carrying a nearly overflowing basket on her back, supported by a headband of braided coconut fibre. She looks terribly fragile to us. We can hear a faint, shy *Namaste* coming from her lips. We are overwhelmed by this everyday scene of human hardship and its quiet acceptance. It is particularly emphasised by the inclement weather conditions; we feel humbled and we know that we will never forget this image.

All of a sudden, we are interrupted in our contemplation. A herd of mules — the leading animal carries a big noisy bell — appears through the flurry and, seconds after, disappears again on the far side of the pass.

We start our descent to the north, in the direction of Junbesi, and soon enter the tree line with mixed growth. A massive snow squall is brushing the leaves off the trees and bushes, creating the sound of a huge waterfall roaring nearby. Although I keep telling myself that they are used to it, I feel great sympathy for our porters with their poor footwear and primitive clothing. We have to be careful that no one slips on the slippery rocks. A pulled hamstring or a broken ankle would be fatal now. For days our umbrellas have been left tied to our backpacks, unused, ridiculously. Today the umbrellas are keeping the worst of the showers off and perhaps, preventing a cold, definitely worth the money we spent on them in Jiri. I can still see my friends that day, grinning from ear to ear. They are not laughing *now*.

A swarm of jackdaws indicate that we must be in the vicinity of houses. Indeed, they appear just behind the forest, out of the fog. In a warm and cosy *bhatti*, we sip our hot lemon while, outside in the courtyard, our instruments in their plastic sheets are putting on little white hoods. If only the weather would improve! The closer we get to the valley of Junbesi, the more the snow turns into rain and, finally into thick clouds of mist, behind which ghostlike, treetops, hide. For a while we hike along mogul-shaped, sloping meadows, then finally we can see the first roofs of Junbesi. Beeker has to lie down immediately. Boosted by today's weather, his cold has broken out fully. We give him a strong dose of pills. The rest of us are also exhausted from this strenuous day's march. I have a headache and am longing for dry clothes.

Our accommodation today is spacious. Gyaltsen has already ordered dinner for us. For a change, we are having potatoes with vegetables and lots of hot lemon and *chiya*, the Nepalese milk tea. We are sitting on rough wooden benches covered with foam rubber. After dinner we pick up our instruments for tuning. Surprisingly, my dulcimer has kept its pitch, matching that of Erich's accordion. Cups are being passed around, along with a big thermos of milk tea. All available seats next to the big buckets filled with red-hot embers are soon occupied by smiling villagers. They are mostly dressed in warm brown robes. The women are adorned with coloured stone necklaces. Several of the men, with a murmur or with a peculiar nasal sound, are counting their prayer units by running rosary-like strings of wooden beads through their fingers; *Om mani padme hum.*

Erich gives the beat. First a Bavarian piece, as usual; later the Nepali songs, which are always the highlight. It is the sixth time that we are playing them here in Nepal; every time we play more harmoniously. The people follow our performance very attentively. They are surprised that foreigners would travel from as far as Germany, with their instruments, to Nepal to play music in their villages. Of course, they had heard that we had come to play for Gyaltsen's sixtieth birthday, but they still see it as an extravagant undertaking. We feel rewarded for that tonight, in this dark Sherpa room, lit only by the warm light of a Petromax.

Gyaltsen translates all questions with ease. He obviously enjoys being in the limelight. We look at beaming faces all around, especially, as *Resham Firiri* resounds. To our surprise, one of the Sherpas leaves the group and finds a space to dance along to the music. The local villagers clap their hands to the rhythm, *Resham Firiri, Resham Firiri.* Encouraged by the dancer, a young boy steps out and plays his version of *Resham Firiri* for us on a small flute that resembles a piccolo. Andi films the impressive event; now it is our turn to ask for an encore. Overwhelmed by his unexpected success, he blissfully plays once more: *Resham Firiri.*

Most traditional songs in Nepal consist of an endless series of verse and refrain. *Resham Firiri* is one of these; an old song which everyone knows. Foreigners who walk into the snowy mountains can hear the song performed by the Gandharvas, the traditional musicians.

First the man starts singing:

Refrain:	Resham, let us fly, Resham, let us fly,
	Up, into the mountains there let us sit down.
	Resham, let us fly.

First verse:	With a single-barrel gun, a double-barrel gun
	aiming at the Muntjak deer.
	I am not aiming at the Muntjak
	But I am calling to my beloved.

| Refrain: | Resham, let us fly . . . |

Second verse:	As one calls the dog 'kutti, kutti',
	and the cat 'suri',
	I implore my great love;
	I wait for you at the crossroads.

Refrain:	Resham, let us fly . . .

After that, the girl sings:

Third verse:	Oh God! A little calf is on the mountain cliff,
	I cannot leave you
	so dear let us go together.

Refrain:	Resham, let us fly . . .

Fourth verse:	Millet was sowed, corn was sowed
	but paddy was not sowed.
	Do not follow me,
	I do not want you.

Refrain:	Resham, let us fly . . .

Here follow three more verses by the girl, then a verse by the man, who says he will die if she does not come to the cross-roads. The girl takes pity on him, does not hide anymore and meets him at the crossroads. In the end she falls in love with him after all.

In Nepali the song goes as follows:

Refrain:	*Resham firiri, Resham firiri.*
	Udeyra jaunki, dandaa ma bhanjyang,
	Resham firiri.

First verse:	*Ek naaley banduk, dui naaley banduk,*
	mirga laai takey ko.
	Mirga lai mailey taakeko hoeina,
	maya lai dakey ko.

Refrain:	*Resham firiri, Resham firiri . . .*

Second verse:	*Kukur lai kutti kutti,*
	biraalo laai suri,
	Timro ra hamro maya ra priti dobato ma kuri.

Refrain:	*Resham firiri, Resham firiri . . .*

Third verse:	*Saano ma sano gaiko bachho bhirai ma, Ram Ram.*
	Chodera jana sakin mailey,
	baru maya sangai jaun.

Refrain: *Resham firiri, Resham firiri . . .*

Fourth verse: *Kodo chharyo, makai chharyo,*
                    dhaan chhareko chhaina.
                    Pachi, pachi na aau Kanchi,
                    manpareko chhaina.

                    Resham firiri, Resham firiri . . .

Master Sherpa E. Niethammer

Jochen 'Erich' Abel

'Either you conquer the mountain or, the mountain conquers you.'
— Master Sherpa E. Niethammer

Words of wisdom, from the lips of our cameraman Eberhard
Niethammer, were to provide entertainment today. Wake-up
call is at 6 a.m., as usual, then breakfast. The compulsory *puris*
with jam, *chiya*, and of course a cigarette, will get us ready for
the mountain.

Because the batteries need recharging, we can forget
about videotaping today. M.S.E.N., therefore, is walking without the tripod, which is normally casually thrown over his
shoulder. Instead, he carries the camera case skilfully, in
Sherpa manner, with the strap across his forehead. All are
ready and off we go, uphill. The sun is shining today. M.S.E.N.
is still in good shape after his most important meal of the day.
Through the binoculars, we look back to Bhandar. The
French women, on our route since yesterday, pass by.

First stop: *Chiya*. 'Hot Showers' are advertised. 'It's all a
swindle', Ebi enlightens us, taking a picture of a window at
the lodge with his digital camera. He forgets about the strap
around his forehead; while leaning back, the camera slides

off. With a masterful reflex, he catches it and puts it back in its original position.

It is getting cooler as we move higher. I meet an Englishman, in shorts, who raves about the excellent food in Junbesi, our destination. There is also a bakery.

At an elevation of 3,100 metres, I hear birds chirping; for a second, I see a monkey jumping from one tree to another. Gyaltsen confirms that there are still two species of monkey at this altitude. M.S.E.N. remarks:

'Yes, at a height of about 3,000 metres you start seeing monkeys.'

He really makes me wonder: could it be possible, that I am suffering from altitude sickness, that I am hallucinating?

We pass a group of porters who are taking a break by the roadside. One of them is carrying a load of 80 kg in his basket. It makes me skip ahead like a mountain goat. Short of reaching the pass, we have lunch in a pretty lodge, with *thukpa* and *chiya*.

The cold is increasing, and then there is a soft shower of hail! Finally, the highest point for today is reached; it is decorated with prayer flags. We all throw a stone for Buddha and thank him for the successful ascent with 'soso' (prayer for blessing). From now on it is all downhill, and steep! It begins to snow. It is the first time that I have used my walking stick. I bring up the 80 kg for discussion. M.S.E.N. explains, 'Eighty kilos sounds like a lot, but the right carrying technique is the key!'

The snow turns into rain further down, but just before our arrival at Junbesi, the sky clears. It is a larger village. The bakery, unfortunately, is closed.

It is Saturday — which is 'Sunday', the weekly day off, in Nepal. End of dream. Gyaltsen takes us to a lodge run by Tibetans. A group of Tibetan monks are staying there as well. We congregate in the kitchen, which for us is synonymous with a living room. The host has set up buckets with embers.

After we have warmed up, we start our music. The hosts and guests from the neighbourhood are present. We are playing in a very relaxed way today. With *Resham Firiri*, spirits reach a high point and people are dancing until the cook signals that dinner is ready.

After dinner we sit around socialising. Gyaltsen sits with one of the monks and converses in Tibetan. I am looking forward to my sleeping bag.

> *'Weaklings have big hankies to cry into at night . . . '*
> — Master Sherpa E. Niethammer

From Junbesi to Nuntala

Matthias 'Beeker' Bauche

Gyaltsen wakes us up shortly after six. After we have over-come the shock of the cold and have packed our backpacks, we meet in the soot-black kitchen. The smoke seems to be permanent. It smells of spices which are used to brew the tra-ditional Himalayan milk tea. A few Nepalese greet us with a smile. The morning staff serve us Tibetan bread with jam and tea. While our porters load the instruments into their baskets, Gyaltsen checks the rooms to make sure no one has forgotten anything. Ebi and Andi catch a few scenes on film, then we are off to Solung. We walk along the street which is paved with large natural stone slabs, until we leave the village through one of the typical Buddhist *kanis* (the gateway to the village, like a *chorten* with an archway through its middle). The white *stupa* disappears slowly from our view, as we walk downhill, through terraced fields, into the valley. We are at the Junbesi Khola.

While crossing the river on a daring suspension bridge, we see several colourfully painted mills along its banks. Through a dense forest, the path leads steeply up on to a plateau. Past farmhouses and hamlets, we reach a vantage point, from which we have an extraordinary view over fields and mead-ows, down to Phaplu and its airport. There is not a cloud in

On the road with Dulcimer and Double Bass.

the sky. This helps us to forget yesterday's miserable weather. The warm rays of the sun feel wonderful. We walk for a while on a well-used path which is level, neither up nor down; it is so nice and easy for a change, we could not feel better. A group of children, in blue school uniforms, are walking towards us. Some ask for candy, and Charly digs again for chewing gum. Shortly afterwards, past a bend, we reach the village of Solung and, for the first time, we see the Everest range. I cannot help staring. My hands are becoming all tingly and sweaty from the excitement. Before us, finally, rising into the blue sky, are Everest, Lhotse and Nuptse. Our destination, Namche Bazar, should be lying just at their feet.

We take a rest at a teashop, for some hot lemon. A few of us take photos for a while. Andi and Ebi are filming. A few colour photos surface from the bottom of Charly's backpack. A friend in Garmisch-Partenkirchen had given him precise instructions where, and to whom, to deliver these. The hostess of the lodge is not a little surprised to see her photo, hand-delivered all the way from Germany. It makes her very happy that someone, so far away, remembers her.

Then, it is time to start again, in the direction of Ringmo village. The magnificent view of the Everest mountains remains constant before us. In Ringmo, which lies on the banks of an idyllic stream, we stop for lunch. We have enough time for a cleansing dip in the stream and to wash some of our dirty laundry. Just as we are wondering about Ebi's where-abouts, he arrives. Now we can have our noodle soup. With it, we have plenty of milk tea or hot lemon. Quite satisfied, we continue our trip at a slower pace.

For a while, we follow the valley; this leads to a steep path, towards the 3,071 metre high Trakshindo pass. The easy part of the trek is over. Our conversations are gradually becoming more sparse until, towards the end of our climb, I hear only my own breath. Finally we reach the top. It is quite cold and windy here, with the sun already close to the horizon. We walk through a gate on top of the pass, to which prayer wheels are attached. We turn every single one. We enjoy the impressive panorama on the far side of the gigantic Khumbu Himalaya. Tibetan monks pass, greeting us, *'Tashi Delek!'* Now we have to lose the altitude that we have just gained, hiking all the way down on the other side. Past a monastery and a few hamlets, we descend toward Nuntala, whose striking blue houses we can see from far away. When we arrive, it is already dark.

I am eager to get rid of my backpack. Walking right behind Gyaltsen, I am with him as he turns into a lodge to organise our accommodation. Finally, we can freshen up and have dinner!

Again, it is *dal bhat* tonight, a Nepalese dish of wet rice and stretched lentil soup, subtly spiced with hot radish and chard. Unintentionally, I watch as Ebi looks, full of longing, at a cup-board, which contains canned sausages, tuna and packages of soup mixes. I can hear the grumbling of his stomach across the room. As on most evenings, we perform tonight. The room is packed with villagers, inspecting our instruments with great curiosity. They chatter incessantly. But while we are playing, there is respectful silence, and after *Resham Firiri* an enthusiastic: 'One more! One more!'

At Dudh Kosi — I

Although we still feel yesterday's steep descent from the Trakshindo pass to Nuntala in our bones, Gyaltsen knows no mercy. He is on his feet by quarter to six to provide for all of us. Warm milk tea and bread have to be ready for us by six thirty. Today, we would all have liked to sleep in, just a bit. But a long hike to Bupsa awaits us. Through deepest darkness we hear Gyaltsen's, 'Good morning, breakfast is ready.' From somewhere there is a deep sigh: 'What, so early??'

The Tamang are shouldering their loads, Carolin pays the host and we are ready to leave. Outside, we are surprised by the frost that has covered all green with a silvery velvet coat. Just looking at it makes us shiver. Past Nuntala, this romantic village with well-kept paved streets, stone walls and stately houses, we walk on relatively level terrain, then an increasingly steep path into the valley of the Dudh Kosi. The weather is cooperating; a near cloudless sky, the sun is still low: winter is not far away.

Today's trek reminds me of the valley of Likhu Khola: fertile, a picturesque landscape. We take a short break in the hamlet of Phuleli. The Rai live here, a friendly people, who are extremely hospitable. While preparing tea, they entertain us with Nepali music from a transistor radio.

Rai women adorn and decorate themselves most of all the Nepalese tribes: with various types of rings in their ear lobes, a piece of jewellery to decorate the sides of the nose, called *phuri*. Most characteristic is the *bhulaki*, a ring through the nostrils.

The Rai

Ulrich Gruber

Like the Limbu's, the Rai are a tribe with Mongolian features and a Tibetan-Burmese language. Insofar as they adhere to their traditional way of life, they have a bamboo-based culture. Tools and objects of everyday life are made of this material wherever possible; baskets, containers, mats, trays, stools, brushes, combs, strainers, and even musical instruments. Originally, the houses of the Rai, especially at the upper Arun, were stilt houses, which also were built of bamboo, wherever suitable. Walls and the platform, which rests on poles, are made of a woven bamboo network which is filled with clay. The roof is also covered by bamboo mats, combined with straw. The living area is reached via simple ladders, with notches in their trunks for steps. These stilt houses are becoming scarce, however, because they are increasingly being replaced by easy-to-build rectangular stone buildings. The outside walls of these houses are painted with ornaments for decoration and to fend off menacing spirits.

The Rai are mountain farmers who cultivate their terraces mostly with rice, but also with grain, corn, peas, beans, buckwheat, mustard and millet. The living quarters are usually, surrounded by gardens, supplying vegetables, fruit, and chilli peppers. Their clothing is mostly of wool and cotton and is home-tailored. Their reliance of these mountain people on farming gives them self-sufficiency and independence. All men and boys from age ten onwards, carry the curved Khukri in their cloth belt. The achievements of modern times, particularly the technology of road building, have, little by little, caused the disappearance of traditional stilt houses and are eroding the Rai's self-sufficient, independent way of life.

The religion of the Rai is a mixture of Hinduism, Buddhism and Shamanism, with an emphasis on a cult of elders and demons. Every Rai home has a clay vessel hanging in a corner, in which the house God, Khamang, is worshipped. The Rai form clans, called Thar, which usually comprise a valley community or a group of villages. These larger clans make marriages within a Thar possible; they are quite common, as long as there is no direct family relationship. Three forms of marriage lead to the establishment of a new family. The first is the wedding arranged by the parents, second, the theft of a bride, which is prearranged by the partners and followed by the wedding, and third, simply marriage for love. Relationships between unmarried young men and girls are fairly liberal and there are, usually, plenty of occasions to meet at a shared work place or at festivities. Children are much loved; one can regularly see elder brothers and sisters carrying younger siblings about all day. An extended family, like that of the Tharu in the Terai, does not exist; each young couple strives to establish its own home, after the initial years in the family home.

At Dudh Kosi — II

The longer we are on the road, the more delighted we are with the entire trek from Jiri to Namche Bazar, the more we seem to drop the habits of our 'civilised' world. We are impressed by the warmth of the people, their connectedness to the soil and their piece of earth, where they live. Whatever it is, knitting clothes, drying fruit, sorting grain, ploughing the field, threshing of corn, almost everything is done by hand. The first machine we encounter is an antique manual sewing machine. An old Indian man sits, cross-legged, on the side of the road, sewing with it. I would like to take a picture of him but he refuses, vehemently. To my question he responds with a categorical 'no!' enforced by a sweeping movement of his arm. No room for misunderstanding here!

We are getting close to the Dudh Kosi. We can already hear its roaring from below. A few little streams are running off the Trakshindo, with a fresh, splashing sound. Terraced fields alternate with rhododendron groves; there is the occasional chestnut, holly or oak. Here, in the lower regions, banana plants are cultivated in the vicinity of the houses. Through the roar of the Dudh Kosi, we can sometimes hear a warbler or a bulbul. On a field nearby, a water buffalo, tied to a stake, is licking her calf. The path is busier now, with porters coming down from the Trakshindo or across from the Khari Khola. Their chatter is drowned in the roar of the nearby waterfall.

At a *bhatti*, which is fully exposed to the morning sun, we warm up next to the suspension bridge across the Dudh Kosi.

Suspension bridge across the Dudh Kosi.

As at most stops, we are surrounded by children. 'Give me sweet' — 'what's your name?' They particularly like the 'big guitar'. Although most children in the Himalaya are dressed in poor, torn clothes and usually look dirty, this does not at all diminish their charm and wild beauty.

'Dudh' means milk, 'Kosi' river. Today the river justifies its name by its milky opaque water. From the bridge which is about seventy metres high, we have an impressive view of the rapids of the thundering Dudh Kosi. I stay back to take photos. With the knotty branches of a dead tree in the foreground, I manage to take some fantastic *contre-jour* (back-lit) shots of our porters crossing the bridge. Just as I am finished, a herd of mules trots on to the bridge from the opposite side.

Chiete cannot get out of the way quick enough. One of the animals knocks him off balance and he falls under his load. Fortunately, Malte is close enough to help him back on to his feet. He just grins, 'No problem.' This is one of those moments where I would like to be able to converse with the Tamang. I cannot help thinking how this incident on the bridge might have turned out, had it not had a side rail.

Along steep serpentines, the path leads to a high plateau. We are overwhelmed by the panorama that opens up to us here. Below, on the left, the Dudh Kosi; ahead of us, at the horizon, the icy giants of the Khumbu Himal, and above us, the deep blue sky. We cannot help thinking of our presence here as an incredible gift.

In Jubing, a small romantic village surrounded by green terraced fields, corn fields, gigantic rhododendron and golden brown haystacks, Gyaltsen gives the signal to stop for lunch. We run into the two very pleasant Frenchwomen again, who also stop here for a break. We have met them several times since Junbesi. Sandrine, the younger one of the two, owns a fashion boutique in St. Tropez and works for half a year; during the other half she is usually en route somewhere in Asia. Independence, to her, is a big adventure. Christine is from Annecy, where she works as a hairdresser. She too, travels as often as possible in Asia, for which she takes half a year of unpaid vacation. The two keep a good pace. I am not surprised to hear that they have just done the Annapurna circuit. We enjoy meeting the occasional trekker. Since Jiri, we have only seen eight tourists.

When Beeker hears that we are getting *dal bhat* today instead of noodle soup, he takes two spoons and bangs them to the beat of his new creation: the *dal bhat* blues. 'Dal bhat . . . *dal bhat.*' Some of the guys are turning up their noses. Could this be a sign of discontent, the beginning of exhaustion, which I think I see in some unshaven faces? I do hear some murmur of 'have a day of rest . . . '

The afternoon is marked by yet another picturesque trail. Our path takes us, partly over steps, through tiny romantic villages. A group of women rest their water pitchers on the well. Others are kneeling in front of aluminium bowls, washing laundry; some clothes are spread out over the rocks to dry.

They are deep in animated conversation. Market places and laundering locations play an important role as communication centres. We have noticed that men almost never do household chores. The roles are clear: women tend to the house and family, men are mostly on the road as porters.

The path is becoming more level and leads, in a wide turn, through light green rice terraces. Khari Khola, the next village, is at an elevation of just over 2,000 metres. The village has transformed itself noticeably in the last few years. An abundance of lodges, with imaginative names, and *bhattis* have contributed to its enormous growth. Most of the windows and doorframes are painted light blue, there are only a few in yellow and green. The road through the village is paved; alongside it is the odd little general store. Known all over Nepal is the open-air game called 'carom'. A square wooden board with round holes in each corner is placed on a table. With a flick of the middle finger over the thumb, the players try to shoot blue and white stones into these holes, more or less skilfully and with varying degrees of success.

Gyaltsen is standing next to me and points out three figures coming down from Bupsa. He greets them, *'Tashi delek'*. *'Tashi delek'*, they answer with a contagious smile. Big white teeth shine from dark, elongated faces; the extremely narrow eyes suggest that the men come from Central Asia. I notice the red ribbons braided through their shiny black hair, which, along with the colourful clothes, identify them as Tibetan. Gyaltsen talks to them for a while. Later, he tells me that they are pilgrims, on the way from Nang Pa La to Gompa Thupen Choeling, near Junbesi.

The pilgrims vanish, light-footed, while we attack the last two-hour leg of today's trek. They would prove to be two challenging hours. Looking up the incline, where the fine brown line of our path gradually disappears, I am surprised to recognise Carolin's white sweater. She must have gone ahead with the right idea: bite your teeth and get it over with! I envy her for her head start and for having negotiated that steep portion, which still lies ahead of me. I have great respect for those in the group who are not mountain climbers and yet have kept pace without a problem or complaint.

The rest of us, at the end of the team, the Tamang, Gyaltsen, Malte and I, reach the plateau above, which could not be seen from below, half an hour later. We are perspiring, but not at all exhausted — yet. Andi, our Superman, was up there long before us and has set up his camera leisurely, to film us in action, as we trot up the steep path. It is always nice to catch up with everyone, somewhere nice, to exchange impressions and experiences.

Bupsa lies on the next, higher plateau. There again, we have a panorama that could not be more beautiful. In the south are the houses of Khari Khola and the valley of Dudh Kosi; in the west are the mountains flanking Trakshindo pass. To the north, on the horizon, stand the ice giants of the Khumbu.

As in many lodges, here too, we see an advertisement for 'Hot Shower'. Great idea today! Even though the water is cold, it feels good to freshen up and feel clean. A group of Australians is also staying overnight. They are an appreciative audience along with a few local people, for our musical presentation at the hour before dusk, high above the valley of the Dudh Kosi. As in Bhandar, not many villagers seem to have time for, or interest in, our music but we sense that we are well liked, as are our instruments, which, not unlike the ubiquitous prayer flags, carry the Nepalese tunes into space.

An 'Easy' Day

'Good morning, everybody.' Like clockwork, Gyaltsen is here again! 'It is not so long today, but the sides of the Dudh Kosi are sometimes a little bit steep. Be careful, please.' Smiling, he explains today's terrain from Bupsa to Surkhe.

He cheers us up repeatedly. We follow his example in shedding our early morning lethargy, when we find it difficult to crawl out of bed.

Yesterday's talk of a day of rest is forgotten as soon as we look at Gyaltsen's encouraging face. After a few kilometres of hiking through the beautiful countryside, we are full of cheer again.

The day before, we were passed by some frail but bold looking men. Today, as we rest on the side of the path, they walk by again with their loads, heavy quarters of slaughtered yak and their hides. We can tell by their faces, which are distorted by strained muscles, how hard this labour is. Especially, when the fur pelts in the wire baskets seem extremely heavy. Gyaltsen explains that they are on the way to Namche Bazar's upcoming Saturday market and that they are Hindus without caste, so-called untouchables. They probably spent last night somewhere under the sky.

The Hindus are traditionally divided into four castes, which are further subdivided into two- to three thousand lower castes. Brahmin — priests and scholars — are considered the head of the Hindu society, therefore the highest caste. They are followed by the Kshatriya — warriors. The third are the Vaishya — merchants and farmers; the lowest are the Shudra — workers. The casteless — the 'untouchables', are at the lowest level of the main castes. To be untouchable, originally, meant a life without rights, a life in the shadow of society. The life of an untouchable was worth less than that of a holy cow, it could not be soiled more than it already was; not through working with animal hide, nor through the cremating of bodies, not even through cleaning toilets or the streets. The mere shadow of an untouchable could soil someone of a higher caste. It was Mahatma Gandhi who eventually denounced such inhuman social discrimination within Hindu castes, and helped these casteless to gain more rights.

While we are lost in thought, following the meat carriers with our eyes, they are swallowed by the rhododendron forest, one by one. Shortly thereafter, we also are in this thick, jungle-like forest. Not a sunbeam penetrates the treetops. Rhododendron combines here with hemlock, bamboo, holly, maple and silver fir, which is covered by strands of lichen, to form a black-green thicket. Small brooks run softly over moss-covered rock beds. A sudden turn leads into a steep incline and then to a clearing. From below it looks like a pipe leading into the sky, with live silhouettes of carriers against a movie screen.

In the clearing, we meet two young women in long dresses, gathering dry leaves into their *dokos*, which they then empty on to large piles. *Namaste*, Gyaltsen greets them, and they talk for a while in the Sherpa language. They are laughing. Then they lift their baskets on to their backs, putting the carrying straps around their foreheads, and skip off, light-footed, towards the nearby farmhouse. From the back they look like two big baskets on feet.

In this big clearing, there are only a few bushes among the grass and rocks, randomly lying around. We soak up the early afternoon sun and enjoy this pleasant spot. We have two more hours to go to Surkhe. Our camera team Andi and Ebi, are

Women carrying leaves in a *doko*.

doing some work with our excellent porters. They do not need to be persuaded to be filmed or interviewed. On the contrary, it means a welcome rest for them, and the Sherpa as well as the Tamang are proud to be filmed and to be the centre of attention for an hour. There is a condition attached. Each one has to sing a little song. Unprepared and a bit bashful, they have to think about it. Gyaltsen makes suggestions for some of the many porter songs that he would like to hear, and he translates for us.

Our conversation with the porters usually consists of the few Nepalese words we know, and some grimaces and sign language. Their English rivals our knowledge of Nepalese. More specific or complex information requires Gyaltsen's interpreting. We want to know where they live, do they have families, how do they see their future, etc. We are curious about their life stories, partly, because they lead such spartan and, for us, exotic lives, and also because their lifestyle is poles apart from ours. We, accustomed to the luxuries of western affluent society, are often discontent for no obvious reason. Perhaps we can learn from the lives of such simple people.

The camera team starts with the youngest one, Chiete. Andi holds the microphone, while Ebi films with his Canon. Chiete tells us his age and talks about his father and mother, siblings and his life as a porter. He concludes with a song. It is a love song; and while he is singing, he is laughing so hard that his already slanted eyes are almost invisible. Now his high voice breaks and that is the end of *his* song. We double over with laughter. Then it is Nanpuri's turn, he is the next oldest. He hardly fares better. The same happens with Harka, Asman and Pemba. Nonetheless, we all clap our hands with enthusiasm. Time passes quickly with entertainment. Andi and Ebi are happy with their production.

The interlude has delayed us. The sun is already approaching the mountain crests on the far side of the valley. The path now extremely steep continues to a little hamlet, from which

View of the Kongde Ri mountain.

we have a marvellous view of the majestic, perpetually icy Himalaya. The white peaks of Kongde Ri and Gyachung Kang seem so close, yet it would still take days to reach their foothills. The first houses of Surkhe are visible from a little plateau. The narrow bed of the Surkhe Khola glistens in the low sunlight. Occasionally, typical stone walls line the road. Where it narrows to a path again, there is an abundance of bluebells and asters.

Surkhe now lies in shade and the coloured rooftops appear flat in the dim light. A wooden bridge offers us entry into the village. In a yard on the right, a black pig keeps a flock of chicken company. Children gather around us. Surkhe is a tiny, cosy-looking village. Yellow seems to be the favourite colour here. Balconies, chairs, benches, window frames, everything is painted in an odd shade of yellow. A group of people are fixing a roof. While Andi and Tsewang have continued towards Lukla, to load the battery for the film camera, the rest of us squeeze our luggage into the comfortable, warm lodge. *Namaste.*

Only a Petromax lights the dark kitchen. With flashlights, we search out our simple resting places. We are happy to have potatoes and vegetables again for a change, along with a few bottles of beer. Carolin, Ebi, Beeker and Erich play a round of Skat, (a German card game comparable to Euchre), while Malte, Simon, Gyaltsen and I play a memory game with the porters. A friend of mine, Rolf, has made this game especially for Gyaltsen's sixtieth birthday, using photos of mountain hut life in the Wetterstein. It proves to be the best entertainment after a day of trekking. No one feels up to playing music today. We will do a concert again tomorrow, in Mondzo.

The Suspense is Mounting

We have switched our diet from Tibetan bread, which is like a thick pancake, to *chapatti's*, made of dough similar to our pancake dough, but without salt. It is fried over a fire in a frying pan, into very thin crepe-like pancakes. Fat is used very sparingly; it is too precious. *Chapatti's* do not fill our stomachs the way the at least three times thicker Tibetan bread does. But we feel strengthened for today's march to Mondzo. Tomorrow — we can hardly believe it — we will be in Namche Bazar!

We leave Surkhe via a stretch of stone steps. Our porters left half an hour ago. A very steep portion of the trail, just outside the village, demands the utmost effort from them. Even we work up a sweat. Just past it, we encounter a very early *dzo*-convoy. The high-pitched ting-a-ling of their bells is music to our ears. Tibetan bells sound clearer than, for instance, the yak bells sold as souvenirs at markets, or in Kathmandu, They are made of better material. It is like comparing the song of the nightingale with the twit-twit of the chickadee. The pleasant sound of the bells, the beat of the hoofs, the sharp whistling of the drivers, along with the animals' sounds, blend into a rhythmical tune.

Although our backpacks are not particularly heavy, the straps put pressure on our shoulders. In the meantime, we have a cure for the pain: a short glance at the loads of our porters. At the top of the climb, the fastest of our group are waiting for us. There is a vantage point, laid out with stones, and a few clay houses along the edge. Below us spreads the haze above the Dudh Kosi, towards the south is the flight path of the small planes from Kathmandu. We observe one of them, landing on the stone runway of Lukla.

There are numerous Mani walls along the way; at nearly every tiny little brook, one of the painted wooden prayer wheels is set up. Rusty metal parts are continuously squeaking, inviting us to listen to their monologues: rest friend, take time to meditate. The flapping of prayer flags, the stone tables of the Mani walls, prayer wheels, all these are signs of a practiced, omnipresent religion. They invite us to pause, and give rise to a spiritual feeling, which cannot really be explained rationally; yet travellers carry it home from Nepal, never to be forgotten.

Lukla must be close now, above us. We hear the humming of an aeroplane flying up the valley, preparing for landing. The conditions here require special skills from the pilots. While we are still shielding our eyes against the sun, a second plane is approaching, most probably bringing the next crowd of tourists into the Khumbu. This tells us that, from now on, we may encounter many more people. The quiet days of our trek are behind us.

They were indeed special days and hours. Their true impact may only be assessed and realised many years from now. One thing is certain though: our expectations were surpassed, by far.

In Chauri Kharka, the roads from Jiri and Lukla meet. Here, in the vicinity of the airport, we see a few signs of wealth. The houses are in very good shape and clean, more solidly constructed, the window frames are straighter, walls are painted, and doorframes are all painted in colour. Plain lodges have been transformed into multi-storey buildings, and terraces into sunrooms. Particularly striking is the western clothing local people wear: tracksuits, jeans, *Patagonia* fleece jackets. It is obvious that most Nepalese want to participate in the wealth which tourism brings to the area. It is for the same reason that, besides the Sherpa, Rai, Tamang and Magar are settling here. Lodges and teahouses have become the main source of income, apart from farming and livestock.

Since Junbesi we have not encountered any bad weather or any more signs of winter. Today, we are blessed with a nice sunny day again. We have to drink more, which means we increase the frequency of our *bhatti* stops. Gyaltsen, as always, takes good care of us: *Chiya pinne manbartsaong* (We will drink tea). Hot lemon or ginger tea are our choices. We sit comfortably, now on plastic chairs — these too, are a western influence — and talk with our porters about their favourite songs, which makes us break into loud laughter again. Chiete in particular has a warm and sunny laugh.

Looking at my phrase book I stutter: *'Mo Nepal manbartsu mansche haarn ramrochha'*, which I mean to mean: 'I love Nepal because the people are so friendly.' Again the whole group bursts into laughter. We are in such high spirits that we would love to give a concert here and now. But we can't because Andi and Tsewang are waiting for us in Ghat. The porters quickly puff another Camel, then it is time to continue.

On the trek from Lukla to Namche Bazar, there is one picturesque village after another, Choplung, Kyomma, Chumlo — all very lively places with a main street, predominantly paved. There is hardly a climb or descent. We seem to walk, almost weightlessly, along the Dudh Kosi, past vegetable fields. To our left and right are wooded slopes which reach higher than 4,000 metres. Hidden behind them are the highest mountains of the world. Goats and sheep cross our path; men are driving a herd of mules across a bridge. Higher, to the right, a huge field of prayer flags cheerfully waves in the wind.

We meet various groups — Japanese, Australians, Americans, French and Italians. The whole world seems to be on the road, equipped with cooks, porters and tons of supplies. Sometimes, they ask us where we come from and what are we planning to do with our instruments. The 'big guitar' especially rouses curiosity. After a while we have a well-prepared set of answers. Other trekkers, most likely, do the same. As a big, close-knit group, we are self-sufficient. Among ourselves we discuss when, for instance, a porter seems to be carrying excessive weight, or we exchange impressions when a curious bunch of children ask us all kinds of questions, or when we are shocked about the poverty and feel guilty about our affluence at home.

We arrive in Ghat on time. Andi and Tsewang have been waiting for a while. We express an interest in having lunch in the elegant-looking centre of the village, but Gyaltsen insists that it is too expensive; he knows a better restaurant nearby. We assume that the owner of the Yellow Lodge is a good friend. As is the case with many houses in Surkhe, all the wooden frames of the lodge at the end of the village are painted with yellow oil paint. The Yellow Lodge is located right on the main trek to Namche Bazar. Sherpa women walk by, chatting, a shepherd is driving his sheep, a villager carries tangerines in his basket. He sells them at five rupees a piece; the perfect dessert after noodle soup. From the direction of Namche Bazar arrives a group of tourists, tired but happy. They have completed their trek in the Khumbu area.

Phakding, situated directly on the Dudh Kosi, is a favourite rest stop for expeditions, because it is halfway between Lukla and Namche Bazar, and the large camping ground can accommodate any major expedition. Everybody admires the beautiful modern suspension bridge across the river. A replacement for an older bridge, it was built only a few years ago. With its braces and pillars, it is of interest to Andi and Ebi as an interesting background. Mules and *dzos*, with their loads, can often only be persuaded with the utmost patience to step on to narrow bridges like this.

We advance deeper and deeper, into Sherpa country. Buddhist symbols appear more frequently: carved stone tables, granite blocks, Mani walls and prayer flags. As we climb higher, we see fewer bamboo roofs with stones. Now shingle roofs prevail. Stones are only used to secure the shingles.

It is late afternoon; the sun has sunk behind the mountains above Phakding and it is noticeably colder. We are walking on the west side of Dudh Kosi, in the direction of Benkar, Chomoa, and Mondzo. We pass only the occasional solitary old hut, screaming children in a courtyard, an old couple watching from a window. One kilometre past Chomoa, we finally reach the first houses of Mondzo. The whole village looks dark. We have been on the road for a long time today. Again, we have to fight our way through narrow doors with our luggage and, the double bass puts up a fight. A minute ago, we walked by the wild roaring of the Dudh Kosi; now we are enveloped in a cheerful, welcoming homely atmosphere. Quickly, our hostess shows us our accommodation and the simple shower in the courtyard. Gyaltsen is the centre of attention here; he knows everyone.

'What would you like to eat?' he asks in his caring way. 'Potatoes with vegetable or noodles with egg?' Our vote for potatoes is unanimous today.

'Okay, potatoes need a little more time for cooking. So you can play music before. What do you think?'

'Good, we will play now,' declares musical director Erich.

Today's lodge is more spacious than the last three we have stayed at, especially the living room. Plenty of hooked rugs, on the walls and benches, lend it a lot of comfort. A wood stove radiates pleasant warmth. Every available seat is taken by the villagers. The ambience is light-hearted and casual. The news that musicians from Germany will play in the lodge tonight has preceded our arrival. What a colourful and animated group it is that has gathered here in the dim romantic light, sitting and waiting by their steaming *chiya*. Squeezed among the adults are a few expectant, curious children. Gyaltsen is very pleased. Close to his home village now, he can present his friends from Germany to his people. For the 'fiftieth' time now, he tells the story of how the musical trek through Nepal came about. For the n'th time he explains the music.

It is a good thing that my dulcimer is not out of tune, because it would easily take twenty minutes to tune a hundred strings. It can get stressful or boring when people are waiting for you. Erich gives the signal and we start with *In der Schanz*, one of our swinging Salzburg pieces, in a catchy 2/4 beat with nice minor chord passages. After the first few bars we feel that the spirit of the Sete performance is alive again. We play perfectly together. Gyaltsen entices the Sherpas to applaud. He knows that it is an important stimulant for us. There is laughter, loud babble, clapping — the Sherpas are obviously having a lot of fun. The second piece is *Schoenauer Bayrisch*. Erich's solo in the third part seems to appeal to them, too. We end the piece to roaring applause. Sparks appear to have ignited the audience. Gyaltsen explains the programme in detail. He would make the perfect talk show host. 'One more,' he tells us and impresses upon his Sherpa friends that they must remain quiet, so as not to miss a tone. After two more vivacious Bavarian tunes, he announces *Resham Firiri*. Simon and Malte have attached the capo tasto to their guitars, which enables them to play A-flat major simply as G-major. Carolin has moistened the mouthpiece of her tenor horn for more precision in pitch. Suspense! Erich's 'one and two and . . . go!' At the part where the lyrics start, the first Sherpas start singing. Towards the end, the whole room resounds, '*Resham Firiri, Resham Firiri* . . . '

We are all so intoxicated by this experience that we cannot quite grasp the entire scene. Only with time will we become aware of the impact that these unique hours in the lodge of Mondzo in the Khumbu Himal, had on us. Only in retrospect, and with distance, do we now know that this evening was the highlight of our musical trek.

Back to the Sherpa lodge. Contrary to *Resham Firiri*, *Nepali 2* is a deeply melancholic and sad piece. We are not aware of any lyrics for the piece, but it might well be the story of a lost love or a friend gone forever. A serious melody like this, with its stirring minor chords, is very important as a counterbalance. The audience is visibly touched by the mournful song. With more cheering, they react to the third Nepalese song, a swinging 4/4 beat with several solo passages. I am happy that I hit all the right strings in my dulcimer solo. At the outset of our trekking adventure, when we were playing, I had often looked at Erich with a sceptical expression. It was all a beginning, at least for me. In these last days though, we have really got the music together.

While we are still playing, the smell of food mingles with clouds of smoke; we can hear the banging of pots in the kitchen. Time to wrap it up. Erich, Carolin and Beeker offer two, three more pieces of the repertoire of the Stuttgart band. After these, an increasingly loud chorus demands, 'One more *Resham Firiri!*'

'Okay, last one!' Erich declares with his inimitable nonchalance.

From Mondzo to Namche Bazar

Malte Jochmann

I am in our new apartment in Munich, with my brother Arno. My bed is standing on the balcony of the high-rise, an overhang protects me from the falling soot. The ceiling is pitch black. A light hits my eye, on – off – on . . .

I feel around for my sunglasses, on the stool. I put them on and recognise Simon's grinning face behind a headlight. I find myself in Mondzo, warm and cosy, in a warm sleeping bag. For the first time since Jiri, I have not heard the alarm clock. Mr Guitar, before my eyes here, seems to get some sadistic pleasure from tearing me out of my dreams in such a barbaric manner. I peel myself out of the warm down cover and, because I suddenly feel cold, I have to do something about it. Ebi and Beeker are still sleeping in the next room; I happen to have my Metz-Blitz beside me. Through a crack in the wall, I send a few good morning photon quanta into the room to warm them up. But instead of a 'thank you' or a cheerful disco howling, I get a cool 'Hey, cut it out or you'll be in trouble!' from the mouth of our Master Sherpa Ang Ebi.

At six thirty we are gathered in the dining room for the usual *dudh chiya* and Tibetan bread. I have mine with jam, simply because the honey, which is very liquid here, is definitely much quicker than I am early in the morning. There is a little tension in the air, because right outside Mondzo is the border to Sagarmatha National Park. Normally, one needs a special permit for filming equipment; since we could not afford it, we don't have it. We can only hope that the border guards don't see it. Therefore, anything that might look like technical equipment goes into hiding, in baskets and backpacks. Our hosts send us off with a warm and heartfelt farewell. They must have enjoyed last night's concert as much as we did.

The gate to Sagarmatha National Park consists of a cabin where all formalities have to be settled, and a big gate with a guard, carrying a heavy gun to enable him to settle less formal problems less formally. A thought that does not particularly contribute to relax our group. Predictably, just before the gate, Simon gets the jitters — and something else; as if struck by lightning, he scrambles for toilet paper, which is packed in my ISO mat — originally intended to hide the microphone. He throws his backpack to the side of the fence and races to the nearby outhouse. Perhaps, it is only last night's *dal bhat* that did not agree with him. We are glad and relieved when he returns after a short absence. We have passed the border guard without casualties.

The path runs steeply down to the riverbed. A wild and beautiful landscape receives us. Below, in the wide river valley, the water snakes through scree and rocks. One can almost see the river eating away the banks during the monsoon season. The bridge we cross is tied to two enormous, eroded cement blocks. There, the path branches off up the wooded slope. We can see a suspension bridge high above and lofty. Below me is the thundering Dudh Kosi, the milky river that was named for its permanently greyish, opaque colour. It is the main run-off for the gigantic Khumbu glacier at the foot of Mount Everest.

We are not far from Namche Bazar, where Gyaltsen's home is, and where we will stay and rest for a few days. At a resting spot, along the steep path, two small figures appear suddenly,

Gyaltsen's grandson Dawa.

running toward us from above, laughing. They are Gyaltsen's grandson Dawa and a servant. The timing is perfect; as if they had known when and where we would have our last break. They have brought a thermos with milk tea and glasses for us. I enjoy the tea while Dawa incessantly and cheerfully babbles in Sherpa. Although unintelligible to me, the two instantly provide a wonderful, cheerful atmosphere. Gyaltsen is obviously overjoyed and proud to be able to show off his grandson. Something else is fascinating about this place. We have discovered that, at a particular spot, through a hole in the tree cover, we can see a massive dark pyramid. It is covered with an eternal snowfield — Mount Everest.

The absolutely last leg to Namche, is managed easily and quickly. From a huge boulder alongside the path, we have a magnificent view of this largest settlement of the Sherpa. With houses built into the mountain slope, on large terraces, it looks like an enormous amphitheatre. The style of the houses with their gabled roofs, which look so much like ours, surprised me on my previous trip. They could be standing in a

Swiss mountain village. At the foot of the village, where it is more level, is a large *stupa*, adorned with plenty of prayer flags. Gyaltsen points out his house, the one with the bright green roof. We are almost there. At the entrance to the village a sign says: 'Namche Bazar, 3,446 metres. Come as a guest, go as a friend'. Next to it is the house of Gyaltsen's sister and her husband, where we are already expected.

We can tell by the faces of the porters that they are happy to have reached their destination. They are sitting there happily, sipping their well-deserved tea and enjoying the sunshine. Asman, in his newly acquired flip-flops, maintains that these are the best footwear for a trek like the one we have just completed.

We pass the washing area of the village, which every day, as soon as it is warmed up by the sun, is crowded with men and women. And finally, we enter Gyaltsen's house. The first floor has a large living area. We celebrate our arrival with a delicious lunch, which his younger daughter has prepared for us. Finally we have arrived at the place where Charly made the acquaintance of Gyaltsen six years ago. There are two major impressions of Namche Bazar which I will always remember: the many Tibetans who have pitched their tents on the undeveloped terraces, to sell goods that they have carried here from their homes; secondly, the bakery with the familiar sounding name 'Hermann Helmer', where one can have an authentic Black Forest gateau. We are glad that we have chosen a time of the year which sees relatively few tourists. During the main season it must be crazy. Presently, and every year, there are at least five new lodges under construction. I stroll leisurely through the streets and alleys. Everyone is eager to offer me the whole assortment of their goods, for instance, old, or old looking, Tibetan tools, utensils and jewellery. On this first day a pair of warm socks will have to do; I don't need anything else for the moment. I will have plenty of time to explore this charming place.

Arrival at Namche Bazar.

In the evening, we do some decent jamming in a small circle of friends, out of sheer joy that we have finally arrived. The big birthday concert in honour of Gyaltsen is planned for another day.

The Sherpa

Ulrich Gruber

Venturing into the highest and remotest mountain regions of the Himalaya, close to the border of Tibet, one encounters the third group of the Nepalese mountain people of Tibetan origin. They are closely related with their neighbours in the north by language, religion and culture. There are active economic ties with the Tibetan highlands, which continue to the present day, if somewhat reduced, despite Tibet's annexation by China and the Chinese Cultural Revolution.

The best-known group of people with Tibetan roots are the Sherpas. About 450 years ago, their ancestors migrated from eastern Tibet into the valleys south of Mount Everest. Initially, they settled in the Khumbu, directly at the foot of the Eight-thousanders, but later ventured further into the area of Pharak, east and west of the Dudh Kosi river, and lastly to Solu, an enchanting and gentle forest country. This is where the large Sherpa villages were founded and where the four oldest and most respected clans, the Minyagpa, Thimmi, Chakpa and Serva, settled. Today the Khumbu area could be considered the gate to Sherpa country; the Solu, however, is the true nucleus of the Sherpa people. A few Sherpa groups ventured even further west, to Rolwaling, the land around the Bigu monastery, and to Helambu, north of Kathmandu.

Sherpa villages usually feature stately houses; slightly smaller in the Khumbu and large, with several storeys, in Solu. With the exception of the Newars, the Sherpa have arguably the finest houses of all tribes. On the lowest floor of these houses would be stables and rooms for farming equipment; above are the living quarters. A special feature of Sherpa houses, which is missing in other tribes, is simple toilets that are attached to the living area. Human waste is mixed with leaves and used as fertiliser. The kitchen and community room, with the usual small chapel behind it, are on the upper floor. In a pit in the wooden floor, which is laid out with clay, burns the open fire; the smoke draws freely through the roof and protects the beam structure of the ceiling against vermin. At the fire pit stands a low, wide bench for the master of the house and his guests. Along the walls are shelves for chests and shiny copper and brassware, which show the wealth of the owner. The living room is also the bedroom.

During festivities, arrangements for a stomping dance place men on one side, women and girls on the opposite side. Into early morning hours, the felt boots drum their beat on the floor with such power that the walls shake and the dust flies. During periods of rest, a bowl of *chang* is passed from mouth to mouth. Their hospitality is proverbial, and when invited to a Sherpa home, it is understood that one takes part in the affairs of family life and festivities. Sherpas are traditionally farmers, cattle breeders and merchants. Living at altitudes between 2,200 metres and over 4,000 metres, their farming is mostly limited to growing barley, wheat and potatoes, the latter being particularly important. The main nutrition consists, however, just like in Tibet, of *tsampa*, a coarse wholemeal mix of ground wheat and barley, which is first roasted in hot sand. Salted butter tea, mixed with milk and served like a steaming consommé, accompanies the *tsampa*. Another important beverage in the life of the Sherpa is *chang*, a lightly alcoholic, mead-like drink, made of fermented grain.

A farmer ploughing with a yak.

It is not only served at celebrations and dances, but also has a function in certain rituals. The pre-wedding, which is to prepare the couple for the later wedding, is called 'Dem-chang'. The presentation of a large wooden flask filled with *chang* is the central ritual of this celebration.

The most important animal of the Sherpa farmer is the longhaired, very undemanding yak, which in this area, is crossbred with mountain cattle. Some Sherpas operate farms that resemble our traditional alpine farms.

A part of the family spends the summer with their herd of yak in the higher regions, just below glaciers and snowfields. There, they live in simple huts erected with dry stone walls, covered with bamboo or yak-hair blankets. The cattle feed on the alpine pastures. They milk them, churn butter and also have their festivities. At some time in October, the cattle are driven down into the valley again.

The religion of the Sherpas is Tibetan Buddhism mixed with elements of Bon and Shaman rites. Peace and sympathy, which also show in their treatment of animals, are expressions of the Buddhist philosophy of life.

Originally, the entire Sherpa population followed the orthodox line of the Nyingma-pa, the so-called Red Hat school. After the occupation of Tibet by China however, many Geluk-pa lamas, Yellow Hats, have found refuge in Sherpa villages and have influenced religious life there over the last few decades.

To help preserve the ancient rites and ceremonies of the original Sherpa religion, a monastery was recently founded and established in the vicinity of Junbesi, with the financial help of the German partnership 'Friends of Nepal'. There, young Buddhist monks, aside from regular subjects, are instructed in the old traditions. Every village in Sherpa country has its gompa, the temple. Several large monasteries have become well-known in the western world, through climbing expeditions, travel writing and reports from tourists, among them, the gompas of Bigu, Tschiwong, Mobung, Thami and, especially Tengboche in the Khumbu, at the foot of the Everest massif. The main building and the temple of Tengboche was destroyed in 1989 by a fire, caused by an electrical fault. It was soon rebuilt with international financial help, in particular, that of mountaineering associations. One of the most impressive experiences of any trek through Sherpa country is the privilege to witness a service in a gompa, with its sombre choral recitations and the thundering sounds of the orchestras, consisting of cymbals, shawms and kettledrums. At least as interesting are the magnificent masked dances of the Mani Rimdu festivity.

Sherpas are tolerant and patient, and in their love relations casual and generous; premarital relations are accepted, even marital unfaithfulness and divorce are treated with great leniency. Like all mountain people, Sherpas are dedicated to their children. It is considered a great sin to cause a child to cry or, to beat one. With employment as sirdars (Nepalese team leaders), personal travel companions, mountain guides and cooks, the Sherpas have opened up new professions for themselves in the trekking business. This development started when the first mountaineering expeditions engaged Sherpas as high altitude porters and for roped climbing parties into the highest ice peaks.

Their reliability, intelligence and incredible capability to function at high altitudes make them indispensable companions on high alpine expeditions in the Himalayas. Those same qualities later opened up to them preferred positions as guides for trekking groups. Today, one can hardly imagine any of these without the Sherpas' readiness to help and their acceptance of hardship. Trekking has the advantage that it is not dangerous, compared to the extreme climbing expeditions, on which many enthusiastic young porters have perished in the past.

Weekend Market in Namche

Simon Neumann

Today is market day in Namche Bazar. From Gyaltsen's home we are watching the early morning preparations and are looking forward to the colourful hustle and bustle. Weakened by various ailments, some of us are only marginally participating in today's activities. We leave together but get separated in the crowded market, which spreads over several terraces. Because of our height, compared with the Nepalis, we cannot really get lost in the crowd; nevertheless, it does not seem to be of advantage to Carolin. It still takes her half an hour to fight her way through to a farmer, with the help of her elbows and a loud voice, to buy some yak butter and cheese. Together, Carolin and Erich, who has carried his special spatula all the way from home for that very purpose, plan to make real Swabian 'Spaetzle à la Nepalese' for dinner tonight.

While strolling from one market stand to another, I recognise some of the porters we met along the trek. It is near unimaginable hard work that these porters regularly perform in order to make a living by selling tangerines, chard, toilet paper, soap, batteries, textiles, beer, almost anything, here at the market. I also see a couple of our porters who are helping friends with their selling. On the highest terrace are the butchers, offering large cuts of meat, spread on a blanket and exposed to the sun. If there is agreement between buyer and vendor, the desired quantity is cut off with a knife, which looks like it could do with some cleaning. I wonder if the health department — if there is such a thing — would sound the alarm at the sight of this. From experience I can say, however, that the meat tastes excellent, if a little tough.

A few Tibetan vendors, who have been camping in nearby tents for close to a week, offer clothes and carpets from China. Tibetans are people — in my view — who are hardly surpassed in natural wildness. They are tall men with striking features, weather-beaten skin and eyes which seem to glow. Their long black hair is, tangled with red cloth and jewellery, tied together on top of the head. Clothing is often a sheep or yak hide, with the fur worn inside — not high fashion but appropriate here.

When negotiating, they stay completely calm. While Nepalese appear temperamental when they are haggling, the Tibetans simply indicate with a light movement of the head whether they are content with the offer or not.

Should a potential customer be too unreasonable, a flicking of the hand, along with an ominous growl, and there is no deal. Personally, I only bought some fruit at the market, and mostly absorbed the atmosphere as an outsider. I do not want to carry souvenirs back to Kathmandu, where they might be even more reasonable.

Sherpa Gyaltsen's Sixtieth Birthday

Malte, Andi and I have come down with a cold, first an unannounced shiver, then a strange sensation under the skin and eventually a relatively high fever of 40°C. Why now, just in time for Gyaltsen's birthday party? One by one we crawl into our sleeping bags to sweat it out. I repeatedly fall into a deep sleep, wake up again, bathed in sweat, shivering. In the morning Gyaltsen brings me hot water. He also pours fresh water in small silver bowls at his Buddha shrine. This ceremony, which he celebrates every morning, represents the water absorbing everything unclean during a day. In the evening he throws the water out. He does this with great devotion while murmuring, *'Om mani padme hum'*; somehow, it feels reassuring. In the afternoon I feel better, but Andi is completely down.

The whole extended family in Namche Bazar is invited by Gyaltsen. All of 20 December 1998 is marked by preparations for the festivity. His daughter Serki carries out the bulk of the work and does not leave the kitchen all day. As far as I have understood, there are also preparations and cooking going on in the kitchens of his relatives.

The sun shines through my bedroom window. I suddenly become aware that everyone seems to have left the house, except for the patients. Andi is still deeply buried in his sleeping bag; Malte is just trying to get up. He is totally dishevelled but says he feels better. So, he too, has escaped the grip of the Namche fever. Late in the afternoon, I get out of the sleeping bag. I feel much better and pick up my dulcimer for a tuning. The party is supposed to get underway about six o'clock.

Rather crestfallen, Andi says goodbye. For the time being, he is moving into the house of Gyaltsen's eldest brother, where it will be more peaceful and he can get a good night's rest.

The first invited guests arrive. Gyaltsen's eldest brother with his wife, imposing people, grey-haired, with friendly faces. Not all Sherpas seem to accept turning grey easily. Gyaltsen, for instance, is quite vain and has his hair dyed black every six weeks.

Suddenly, a whole bunch of newcomers arrive together: his sister with her husband, his eldest daughter with her husband and children, two nephews with their wives. The room is full now; twenty-three people altogether, including us, are here to celebrate. He does not know his exact date of birth, but says that it is between August and December of 1938. Perhaps this uncertainty is the reason that birthdays are normally not celebrated here. Or perhaps birthdays are not important enough to keep track of. Today's celebration is, more or less, happening because of *our* initiative.

We are sitting comfortably in a half circle around the stove. Gyaltsen gets up for his speech. Obviously proud, he introduces all his friends from Germany to his big family and emphasises again, that we did not just talk about an idea of a musical trek, no, we actually did it! He elaborates even further, how we met; his six summers at the Reintalanger Hut. He points to the photos, which are casually stuck in the glass panels of the cupboard, showing him in action at the hut, as well as our excursions into Switzerland, Italy and France. He talks about the successful Mount Everest ascent, about two of his brothers who perished on expeditions, and about his wife Gyalmo, who passed away so unexpectedly and too young, in the April of 1993. At this point, his voice trembles and he quickly moves on to today, a more festive time, his milestone birthday; he wishes everyone a cheerful evening and a good appetite at the feast to follow later.

First, though, he asks us to play a few pieces. We will present the Bavarian folk tunes before dinner; the Nepalese songs will follow after the meal. It is so quiet in anticipation, one could hear a pin drop. We begin with the *Schanz*. The children are sitting in the front row so they don't miss anything. The family is spread out over chairs and benches. Here and there, we see a Buddhist prayer string running through fingers. As we end a piece, they are put aside so the owners have their hands free for clapping. The *Schoenauer* ends the Bavarian series.

Then dinner is served — and what a superb feast it is! Gyaltsen's daughter's feast is fit for a king. A delicious aroma rises from porcelain bowls, steam puffs out of copper kettles; aluminium pots sizzle. Certainly, we expected a birthday dinner, but not a fantastic feast like this. It is a cornucopia of *momos* (similar to samosas or turnovers), meatballs, fried yak meat, ground chicken in chilli, fried potatoes, French fries, steamed rice, beans, chard and coleslaw. Sweet tangerines are the dessert. There is also plenty to drink: whiskey, beer and traditional *chang*. For those who don't want alcohol, there is milk tea and hot lemon. Everything is prepared with a lot of care and love; nothing looks plain or half-hearted.

While sampling all the delicacies, we talk to the relatives. We hear that there are other family members who live abroad. Gyaltsen's younger brother and his wife run a successful computer business in Chicago. The feast is in full swing. The conversation is in Sherpa-Nepali, English and German. Above all conversation rises the screaming of children, the barking of Tashi, the Tibetan dog, and the clashing of dishes and silver.

After a last tangerine, we pick up our instruments again. Ebi leads into *Resham Firiri*. The Sherpas listen attentively, then start humming along. If not before, we are certain now that we have won over the hearts of the local people. We wish it were possible to freeze these moments in time. But, as ever, everything is fleeting and ends in memory. This evening in Namche Bazar will remain a very special memory.

Toward the end of the concert, Beeker has his own numbers: *Tulips from Amsterdam* and *My Father was an Appenzeller*. The audience bursts into laughter and when Carolin tops it up with a tenor horn solo, wild applause erupts. Gyaltsen starts telling of the daily wake-up music at the Reintalanger Hut. And this is the piece we choose, to complete the evening for Gyaltsen: *Summer Roses*, an exhilarating but pensive waltz by Hans Dondl, a zither virtuoso from the twenties in Munich. But there is no end in sight yet.

As on other occasions, the audience wants another *Resham Firiri* and we gladly oblige. Between chords, we lift our glasses to toast Gyaltsen one more time: 'Happy Birthday to you!'

It is time for the guests to return home. While we all part with a thankful *Namaste*, each of our group of five receives a *khata*, draped around our neck. These are white, approximately one-metre-long silk shawls which are embroidered with the letters of the mantra, *'Om mani padme hum'*. The shawls will bring us good fortune, health and a reunion. We are overwhelmed by this simple and wonderful gesture, which seems almost like a ceremony, and stand in silence for some time, while Gyaltsen accompanies his guests to the door.

They disappear into the dark alleys of Namche Bazar in various directions.

Christmas in the Khumbu

The morning after the birthday party, Andi shows up; he is feeling better. But now, it is Beeker's turn to be under the weather. Not even the rice pudding, which Gyaltsen has prepared especially for breakfast, does the trick. And he wants so much to walk to Lobuche with us. From there we want to climb Kala Pattar. It would be the first Five-Thousand Peak for Beeker, Simon and Malte. The rest of the group, Carolin, Erich and Ebi are planning to return to Lukla to fly back to Kathmandu, where they want to spend some time and just relax. Today too, we have split up. While the non-climbers are on a hike to Tengboche monastery, we stay behind to just hang out in the sun and, eventually prepare our backpacks for tomorrow. Andi films an interview between Gyaltsen and me. It is for recording the story of our meeting and friendship.

It is spring-like during the day. We enjoy doing nothing for a change and feel that this can be one of the finest irrelevant things in the world. Late in the afternoon, I plod leisurely up to the lookout point near the Sherpa Museum of Namche Bazar. The view from here is overwhelming. Below me is the horseshoe-shaped village; beyond the Kongde Ri, in the northwest rises the sacred mountain of the Sherpas, the Khumbila. Leaning against its right shoulder is the ice-packed peak of the Tawoche. Then the dominating dark grey wall of Nuptse and Lhotse, above which the snow-covered triangle of Mount Everest shines. In Nepali language it is called *Sagarmatha*, 'Mother Goddess of the Universe', in Sherpa and

Ama Dablam

Tibetan, *Chomolungma*, 'Mother Goddess of the Winds'. The icy peaks of Ama Dablam, Kang Taiga and Thamserku, which rise to the right of the valley of the Dudh Kosi, reflect the last light of the day. There is hardly a breeze, and not a sound. I am alone. I cherish the last hour of the day.

On the following morning, the time of departure has arrived. Beeker's condition has worsened; he is unable to climb with us. Instead, he will return with the others to Lukla and fly back to Kathmandu. For our farewell, Gyaltsen has presented a gourmet breakfast: pancakes and boiled eggs, and, as always, milk tea.

The 'big guitar', tenor horn and accordion still have to be packed. We are all assembled in the courtyard in the morning

Thamserku

sun. Before we part, Andi and Ebi take a few more shots of the farewell scene. Gyaltsen presents the Kathmandu travellers with another *khata*. There are long handshakes and thanks for the wonderful adventure and shared experience. I can see and feel that everyone is quite emotional. *Namaste!*

The porters — this time only two, Asman Tamang and Manpuri Tamang, pick up their baggage, and Carolin, Erich, Ebi and Beeker their backpacks, and they are off through the narrow wooden door. We wave after them until they pass the white *stupa* at the washing area; they disappear with the descending path.

Shortly afterwards, we also shoulder our backpacks. Concerned for us, Gyaltsen wants his son-in-law Tsewang to accompany us. He wishes us all the best of health and good weather for the next few days. It is supposed to stay quite pleasant into the Christmas days.

Soon we reach the upper end of the village, through narrow alleys, past the many typical Sherpa souvenir shops. From there, we can see the trio again: Everest, Lhotse and Ama Dablam. We walk energetically, as if we had never been ill. Not to mention Simon and Tsewang, who are fit anyway.

A dusty, light brown path leads us more and more steeply down to Phunki Teng, where the Dudh Kosi and the Imja Khola meet. We rest briefly beside a monastery-like building, from which we can hear the deep, monotonous chorus, murmuring prayers: *Om mani padme hum*, interrupted a few times by a brass bell.

We have barely resumed our hike when we encounter a black yak, which appears to be dying, lying right beside the path. It is twisting and rolling its eyes, and the terrible groaning sends shivers down our spines.

'What do you think is wrong with it?' Andi asks, shocked. 'It could be something like twisted or obstructed bowels. We can't help. And no one will relieve it from its suffering. Only specifically authorised persons are allowed to kill animals.' When Sherpas buy meat, they let it dry for a long time to make sure that the meat is pure; otherwise it might anger the gods.

A little lost in thought, we continue, walking into the day. The Dudh Kosi sends its eternal tune into the air. Vultures are circling above us, a caravan of yaks trots by, undisturbed by us. Rarely do we meet a trekker. In Phunki Teng we rest under an arbour. Since we have not had noodles for a while, we order Chow Mein vegetables for lunch, at the lodge right beside it.

A group of Japanese tourists are sitting in the lodge. Everyone is eating the same food.

We hear the squeaking of axles of prayer wheels nearby. Until lunch is ready, we have time to investigate these barrel-like wooden constructions.

'Not bad, you can have the praying all done for you here,' Simon says.

We are thrilled that it is so pleasantly warm and, after lunch, we stretch out on the benches before we are off again. Up the path, through white spruce, fir, birch and berberis, we continue towards a glade, gradually steeper to an altitude of 3,800 metres. There, where the path seems to end, Simon and Andi are expecting us. From a distance Andi shouts, 'What an amazing place!' Indeed, when I came here for the first time in 1993, the scenery simply took my breath away. The peaks of Kongde Ri, Tawoche, Nuptse, Lhotse, Everest, Ama Dablam, Kang Taiga and Thamserku seem to form the backdrop to a small stage with the Tengboche monastery in the foreground.

This fantastic spot is, rightfully, considered one of the most beautiful and impressive places on earth. On the left of a gently sloping meadow, the monastery spreads out, already in its second reincarnation. It was once destroyed by an earthquake and, a second time, by fire. Tengboche is surrounded by a belt of Himalayan white spruce and enormous rhododendron, broken by a few bamboo patches and birches. To the right of the expansive meadow, where the path from Phunki Teng joins, a *chorten* awaits the trekker, along with ancient granite prayer tables and prayer flags, attached to long wooden poles. For centuries Sherpas have been putting up these prayer flags. They fade with time, but fresh and colourful ones are always added. This perpetual flapping of the flags, against the scenery of the 8,000 metre plus peaks, lends this spot an aura of timelessness and mystique.

In the Gompa Lodge, one of several lodges here, we find

accommodation for the night. A minor headache disappears quickly with an aspirin. It is still early in the afternoon, which gives us time for a stroll to the monastery or the enchanting surroundings. I read Jon Krakauer's book *Into Thin Air*, about the tragedy on Mount Everest in 1996. In the evening, a truly mixed group has congregated in the lodge. There are French, Koreans, Japanese, Germans, Americans and Italians. Everyone crowds around the warm stove. We get our supper of vegetable soup and milk tea faster than expected,. The evening is brutally cold. The whole international trekking community seems to be unable to keep the door closed. Because I am feeling so cold, I finally find some cardboard to use as a wedge to keep the door shut.

The atmosphere of a place just before it awakes, is something very special to me. Throughout the summer, when I wake up at the hut, I step out on to the terrace, to breathe the early morning tranquillity.

Andi and I are up before dawn, to experience the first rising of the day, the loading of the yaks at the far wall of the lodge, and an early morning walk to the monastery. The meadow is covered with frost. The low morning light gives it the appearance of a bluish-grey carpet. The white and black yaks are still lying, dead like rocks, clustered, to keep each other warm. Only their snorting and visible puffs of breath lets you know that they are alive.

While Andi stays with the animals, I walk into the courtyard of the cloister. No signs of life here yet. It is icy-cold in this yard, which is covered in dark grey stone slabs. Along the inside of the stone buildings forming the square is a wooden balustrade. Without making a sound, I walk to the entrance of the main temple and open the door. I barely have time to admire the many works of art, when a deafening drumming sound fills the temple. A monk beats various big brass gongs about fifteen times, with drumsticks. The boom of the first series has hardly faded when the next round resounds. One echo seems to swallow the other. Although it sounds like brutal thunder, destroying the peace of the place, it becomes a powerful presence of something solemn and divine. After that, absolute silence prevails again.

Unsure of what to expect or do, I turn around. In the dim light, the monk, perhaps thirty years old, smiles, as if in response, inviting me to stay and look around. Next to the entrance are three statues, bathed in orange-red light; in the centre is Amida or Jo Rinpoche. To the left a bodhisattva, called Chenresig, and to the right the founder of the Nyingma-pa order Guru Rinpoche, translated as 'the venerable custodian of the treasure'. The side walls are hung with precious, colourful *thangkas*, painted with a variety of *mandalas*. The largest one of these covers the ceiling. *Mandalas*, Buddhist diagrams, symbolise divine infinity within the concept of tantric philosophy.

I am feeling the cold now. Quietly I leave the room to take another look at the courtyard. Ravens are picking at the troughs in the eaves. It looks as if one of them is entangled in a strip of prayer flag. The yaks are now loaded with their burden and they are waiting for the whistles of their drivers. Just as the first rays of the sun hit the frosty meadow, they leave, trotting in step with their long shadows. Soon the caravan is swallowed by the rhododendron forest.

Malte, Simon and Tsewang in the meantime have ordered *chiya* and *chapattis*. Breakfast is over quickly. It is a leisurely five-hour hike to Pheriche. We stop briefly at the house of Ang Kanji Sherpa in nearby Deboche. I stayed at her lodge, near the cloister, six years ago. She is a tall, stately woman, over fifty years old. She seems to recognise me and invites us in for tea.

Just before Pangboche we cross the Imja Khola on a suspension bridge at a dizzying height, which is decorated with prayer flags. We pass the famous *chorten*, behind which Ama Dablam rises into the blue sky like a giant white candle. Staying along the Imja Khola, we pass the hamlets of Chunlungche, Shomare

A *Mandala*

The word *mandala* in Sanskrit is loosely translated to mean 'circle', it is how-ever more than that. *Mandala* diagrams represent wholeness, and can be seen as a model for the organizational structure of life itself — a cosmic dia-gram that reminds us of our relation to the infinite, the world that extends both beyond and within our bodies and minds.

They are a visual aid for concentration and introvertive meditation leading to the attainment of 'Siddhi' — insights and activation of supernat-ural forces. There are many types and varieties of *mandalas* depending on the nature of the central deity.

and Rake; in Ousho we rest for a while. We meet an Italian couple who are heading for Kala Pattar. The woman seems to have a bit of a problem with the altitude. It is warm and we can dry our sweat-soaked shirts and sweaters in the sun. We enjoy a peaceful break, each of us lost in their own thoughts.

It is time to pack up again. We have a constant view of the gigantic south wall of Lhotse ahead of us; to the left the blinding white Tawoche, to the right, the queen, Ama Dablam. We are passing by old prayer tablets and Mani walls continuously; they are decorated with prayer flags. Now the landscape has the appearance of a steppe. Occasionally we see yaks with baggage but hardly see tourists. In Pheriche, we find a clean lodge. A loud group of Englishmen sit around the warm stove in the community room. It is the day before Christmas Eve. We are in great spirits.

The next morning starts slowly. We leave Pheriche at about ten o'clock. Along a little stream, which is partly frozen, we walk towards Lobuche. The terrain is now quite level, with sparsely growing tufts of grass and lichen. We rarely hear a bird up here. Only the gurgling of the stream accompanies us. Ahead, to the left, we can see Cholatse; on the right, a big grassy ridge hides the view of the Lhotse wall. At the close of the valley, the path inclines markedly through a dry bed of rocks until we reach Dughla lodge on the path. This is the only rest for refreshment we allow ourselves before Lobuche. An icy-cold, biting wind has arisen. We quickly get into our down jackets, hats and mittens. On a small plain above Dughla, we stop briefly to take in the atmosphere with the many small *chorten* and prayer flags. The walls of Tawoche and Cholatse look even more imposing from here. The continuation of the path is increasingly rocky, as it leads into the middle of the mighty moraine of the Khumbu glacier. By now, we are at an altitude of 4,800 metres, a record for Malte and Simon. 'You are aware that every thousand metres you reach for the first time, you must celebrate with a bottle of wine,' I explain to them.

'Especially, when you travel such a historical route, which many famous and infamous expeditions have taken.'

On our right we can see the wall of Nuptse again and, far in the distance, where the Khumbu valley ends at a gigantic mountain chain, the Pumori which rises to a height of over 7,000 metres and is known to be dangerous.

Jon Krakauer, in his book on Everest, describes the huts of Lobuche as a cesspool. It may be that the smell of human waste is more noticeable in the spring; however, today, on Christmas Eve, we experience our simple lodge definitely as very cosy. The wind may whistle through a crack here or there, but the little stove, heated with yak dung, takes care of that. Malte turns out to be an ingenious crèche builder. With an Everest postcard as a backdrop, he builds the manger; from scrap paper he cuts an ox and a donkey, Mary and Joseph, and Jesus in the crib. Glue, candles and scissors are part of my emergency kit. It serves us well here. From a piece of carton, which I found lying around, I fashion a Christmas tree. A few tufts of dry grass from outside, for hay and decor — and voila — the Christmas decoration is finished. It looks very good in front of the closed shutter.

Malte and I take a stroll over to the glass pyramid of the Italians, which is a research centre set up by an Italian scientist.

Christmas Eve in Lobuche.

Here, in the elemental world of the Himalayan giants, it looks rather futuristic. The building is sometimes leased by trekking companies. Presently, it is occupied by a group of four Germans who came to celebrate Christmas and the New Year up here.

'You think they might have have wine here?' Malte asks. In the interior of the pyramid we actually find a simple menu. Malte reads, at the top of his voice: 'A bottle of red wine 1,600 rupees.' 'Let's see, that is about 50 Dmarks; but today we can justify a splurge.' It would be interesting to see if they actually have some left. Surprise! Some Nepalese who are cooking up a storm in the kerosene-smoke filled kitchen, come out with a bottle of a dry French red wine. You just have to be lucky sometimes.

'But don't tell anyone, Malte!'

'Will they ever be surprised!' Malte says, excited.

It is almost dark as we return to the lodge. Andi has already ordered noodles with cheese. Tsewang does not feel well. Maybe it is the altitude; we are at a height of 5,000 metres here. Anyway, he does not eat and crawls into his sleeping bag. We have slipped the bottle into a sock, unnoticed, and put it behind the stove to warm up.

'Wouldn't it be great to have a bottle of red wine now with the noodles!? What do you think, Andi?' I ask mischievously. Richard, an Englishman from London, has joined us. 'Wouldn't be bad at all, Charly.' Andi laughs. 'Well, it looks like we will just have to imagine it.' Simon says, sadly, while Malte can barely hide the grin on his face. Finally, the cook serves us four plates with spaghetti and a little pot of cheese sauce which looks like an 'instant' deal to me. Today we will accept anything.

I stand up for my 'long' speech: 'Since we all have to spend Christmas here, without our girlfriends, we should have at least some wine for consolation.' Malte is holding the bottle behind his back and hands it to me. I pull the sock off with a magician's theatrical gesture: 'Voila! Christmas Eve is saved. Merry Christmas, everyone!' Tsewang, who has already gone to sleep, misses the whole thing. But Simon and Andi are grinning from ear to ear and Richard is speechless. Slowly we sip the precious liquid, drop by drop. The light of the candle in the window frame lights up the room and throws shadows of the tiny crib figures onto the shutter. This is quite an unusual Christmas for us. Tomorrow we will have to leave at four in the morning. . . .

Everyone gets out of their sleeping bags quietly. It is bitterly cold. We drink hot tea from a thermos, and have a few biscuits. Then we step out into the cold, clear night and head toward Kala Pattar. Above us, a starry sky is twinkling like a gigantic sea of stars. We stumble forward in the beam of our headlamps, until we find the thinly worn path, up a grassy ridge, then up a higher ridge; it soon turns into a scree, first more or less level, then steep. As we reach boulders, we actually have to do some climbing.

It is so exhausting to move in this cold. The icy wind seems to be on the increase. We definitely want to be on the peak for the sunrise. With great difficulty, do we find our way through the large, loosely stacked granite in the limited beams of our headlamps. The ice-cold wind is blowing mercilessly; we find it hard to communicate. There is a faint sign of dawn, with a huge silhouette slowly appearing on the eastern horizon, the imposing peaks of Makalu and Lhotse and the pyramid of the 8,848 metre high Mount Everest, which surpasses all. Close enough to touch, it seems, their outlines are now clearly drawn against the waking day.

I cannot help but think of Jon Krakauer's book when I see the trademark easterly blowing, long plume of snow off the peak of Everest. We too are beginning to appreciate what icy-cold really means. Malte's toes are already numb. A few more boulders, a narrow strip of scree, Andi is already standing on top, filming, as the rest of us are crawling the last few metres, to the highest point of the peak. We embrace each other and huddle in a close pile, ardently yearning for the first rays of sun. When they finally strike our peak, they are not strong enough to warm us. They are no match for the icy wind, which is getting even stronger with daybreak and robbing us of the comfort the sun could otherwise give us. Malte has had a questioning look on his face for some time now. With his trained eye for geology and geography, he is surveying the surrounding mountains. Then he says matter-of-factly: 'Charly, this peak is not Kala Pattar. It should be further back there, east, near the Everest base camp, there, still lying in the shade.' His stretched arm points to it.

'It can't be, I was up here six years ago,' I react.

'That may well be, but it does not change the fact that we are standing on a different peak.'

For a moment I am utterly embarrassed, particularly when I look at the expressions on the other's faces. No one says a word. Then, trying to save the moment, I state laconically: 'Well, the most important thing is, it is a *peak*, and whatever it is, we may even be a few metres higher!' In fact, back in February 1993, I had thought that this was quite a challenge for normal trekkers, with the two or three more difficult climbing sections. Perhaps I should have realised then that it was the 'wrong' mountain. But then I had come from India, completely unprepared, unacclimatised and without a map. I had had no thoughts beyond my terrible headache and was happy to have climbed a peak, any peak. For me, at that time, this mountain, which we later identified as one of the peaks of Lobuche East, at 5,700 metres, was Kala Pattar. So I was a victim of the same error twice.

Andi films the Everest panorama while we start our descent.

Simon and Tsewang are plagued by a terrible headache, while Malte and I are miserably cold. In spite of that, except for Simon, we decide to climb Kala Pattar. Simon will descend to Lobuche. While ascending on the left side of the Khumbu glacier moraine, the icy wind picks up and reaches storm force. To protect my face, I walk backwards for a while and end up far behind the others. These forceful gusts are wearing me down. Why am I doing this to myself? I am ready to give up. In a still moment I call over to the others that I am turning back. Enough of this! And I am almost positive that Andi, Malte and Tsewang will follow my example and give up too. Relieved, I start my way back to Lobuche and, with the wind at my back, it is hardly any work at all.

Simon is in his sleeping bag when I arrive at the lodge. I am so tired that I too crawl into my bag and fall asleep instantly. My sleep is interrupted by — surprise! — Andi, Malte and Tsewang; they too, have capitulated. With red faces and wild hair, they are standing in the lodge. 'It did not make sense anymore. The wind just blew us over,' Andi explains. What we did not know then is that the Italian couple, whom we had met a while ago at Pheriche, and some other trekkers, had tried to climb the Kala Pattar on the same day, but had given up just past Gorak Shep because of the storm. So, in hindsight, there was a positive side to my error: at least we managed to climb a mountain. Content, we start our descent to Pheriche.

Simon has, for now, lost his enthusiasm for mountain climbing. In Pangboche, he will leave us and return to Namche Bazar and, from there, to Kathmandu. The rest of us decide to make a little detour into the Gokyo valley, via Phortse and Thare. We trace our route back, along the Imja Khola, down to Pangboche. At the fork in the path, we say farewell to Simon. It is the second Christmas holiday.[*] 'Have a safe trip back to Kathmandu. We will see you in a week.'

[*] 'Second Christmas holiday': in Germany, 25 and 26 of December are legal holidays. Stores, offices, banks and government offices are shut down. There is no shopping. 'Boxing Day' would therefore, not be a fitting translation.

In dreamy Pangboche we rest near the gompa. A wind-protected, sunny spot soon lets us forget yesterday's awful cold. Although we still want to make it to Thare today, we take half an hour to look at the famous monastery of Pangboche. Like Tengboche and all cloisters in the area, this is a one-floor square building. It is not as opulent, but considerably older. They say that Pangboche Gompa is three hundred years old. The walls and ceiling are painted with colourful *mandalas* and, as at Tengboche, there are various Buddha and bodhisattva statues. On a wooden panel below is a painted image of the sexual union of a male and female deity, called 'yab-yum.'

To my question, where the yeti scalp is kept, the friendly monk who had let us in answers, with a shrug, that it was stolen six years ago. We thank him with a small tip and a polite *'Namaste'*, and step outside. From here, we have a wonderful view of the Ama Dablam, through a gap between the houses of Pangboche. It is time to get on the road.

Along lofty serpentines, we gradually descend toward Phortse, which is situated at the entrance to the Gokyo valley. Here, we have another view of Tengboche monastery, on the opposite side. Its roof tiles sparkle in the midday sun. In the distance, above, are the peaks of Thamserku and Kongde Ri. Through the haze of the valley shines the silver ribbon of the Dudh Kosi. A few yaks cross our path exactly where it is the narrowest. We know it is up to us to avoid *them*. The shaggy animals stare at us with dark eyes, while passing us very closely.

Andi has picked up the pace again and is already waiting for us down in the valley, where the serpentines end in a level path. His tiny digital camera is always ready to shoot. Phortse lies idyllically among terraced fields in the sun. It is a quiet village. Most people here are involved in farming or animal breeding.

A bit rushed, we have a late lunch in the form of noodle soup and a Coke, which is an absolute luxury up here. From our lunch spot, we can already see the so-called yak trail, winding its way up on the other side of the Gokyo valley. It will be a substantial gain in altitude, but we feel well acclimatised by now. A young Sherpani presents our bill and wishes us 'Good luck!'

Tsewang says, 'Another three or four hours to Thare. I hope the lodge is open.' To be on the safe side, Malte and Andi ask the pretty Sherpani with the long braided hair. With a shy smile, she confirms that it is open. I notice, not for the first time, that Malte and Andi, our two blonde heads, do particularly impress and charm the dark Nepalese. Perhaps it is just that they are younger? Whatever, a little flirting makes for a cheerful atmosphere.

The villages of Dole, Gyele and Lhabarma lying on the left side of the valley, are already in the shade. A little higher stretches the light brown line of the footpath. Our trail is obviously much less travelled, probably because of its exposure. It is treacherously iced over in parts. Through high pastures, deserted in the winter, passing mani walls, we walk a flat stretch until the trail suddenly goes into an endlessly steep incline. On a ridge stands a *chorten* with picturesque prayer flags. Every step reveals more of the gigantic and magnificent backdrop of the 8,201 metre high Cho Oyu, the 'Goddess of Turquoise', lit by the evening sun. Comparatively unassuming, like a brown hill, framed by four lakes, lies our destination for tomorrow, the 5,483 metre Gokyo Peak.

Gokyo Ri

Thare presents itself like an eagle's nest, a simple stone house with several stables, run by two Sherpanis. One is perhaps twenty-five years old, the other about thirty. The younger one is just getting her herd of yaks from the pasture; the older one immediately prepares tea for us. The sun has sunk behind the mountain range of Machermo peak; only the icy flanks of Cho Oyu are still reflecting the evening sun. It is starting to get uncomfortably cold. Until supper, we have some time to read our Krakauer books: *Into Thin Air* and *Into the Wild*, or write in our diaries.

Suddenly, the heavy wooden door opens — two more tourists have arrived. Later, when we introduce ourselves, we find out that one trekker is from Landsberg on the Lech.* His companion is Manbir Tamang, a very pleasant, alert guide. He may be in his early thirties.

The accommodation for the night is quite spartan, but definitely better than a cold bivouac. In the morning, at seven, the first rays of the sun light up the opposite side of the valley. A fire is crackling in the kitchen and tea and Tibetan bread are almost ready for us. At eight we all leave together for Gokyo. The hamlet of Na is our next destination, that is, if this alpine farm is open at all. We feel as light as feathers because it is all downhill from Thare. The Goddess of Turquoise, Cho Oyu, is bathed in the morning sun. The path is rough, it is buried under a scree slope repeatedly. There is

---

* River in Bavaria, tributary to the Danube. Landsberg is a city on the Lech.

only a sparse growth of thin tufts of grass. Eventually it leads into a luscious green river meadow. It is the Dudh Kosi which runs here, still young, in several streams meandering through the pasture, not far from Na. We are lucky; one of the seven huts is open for refreshments. We get a big carafe of hot lemon for the six of us. Manbir Tamang and Hermann, the mountaineer from Landsberg, have decided to join us.

Crossing a primitive wooden bridge, we reach the wide tourist road from Phortse Teng to Gokyo. There is almost no wind here; a few yaks and their drivers are on their way to Gokyo. Further up, we cross the Dudh Kosi again. The path is increasingly steep and I have fallen behind, the others have disappeared ahead. From time to time, I need to walk on my own, at my own pace. I need to stop and look at the surroundings. I am fascinated by Cho Oyu, my dream mountain, with its gigantic South Wall. If I ever try, another eight-thousander, one day, it will be Cho Oyu. Six months before Reinhard Karl was killed by an ice avalanche, at the foot of this mighty south wall in 1981, I had met him in Garmisch Partenkirchen at one of his travel slide talks. I remember well our conversation at the Rassen restaurant, about his best-selling and timeless book *Zeit zum Atmen* (*Time to Breathe*), which had just been published. It represented the excitement and the increased interest in the free climbing scene at the time, like no other book, and became a sort of climber's bible. He was the first one in Germany to make climbing his profession, in the late seventies and early eighties.

I wonder if the Ruddy Shelduck pair is still living at the first of the four lakes. Six years ago, on a forced march from Tengboche to Gokyo, I wanted to stay overnight in Na, but the huts were closed. Night was falling and I was somewhere close to the first lake. That was when I heard the geese. At the time, this was a heavenly sound. I knew that the houses of Gokyo could not be far away anymore, because these geese are so famous they are written up in every travel guide. In the

Prayer flags at Gokyo Ri, with Cho Oyu in the background.

meantime there was a second pair, probably the next genera-
tion. They roam all four lakes several times a day. And then I
did see the first lights of the lodges far ahead on the right.
Completely exhausted from a long day's walk, I asked for a
big supper and, soon after, for a bed. The next day, when I was
skipping from rock to rock at the third one of the lakes, I saw

the duck pair who had given me strength the day before — brown-orange Himalayan ducks.

The lakes of Gokyo are frozen and strange sounds rise from below the ice. The lake has open water in the vicinity of the houses. Passing streams, *chortens*, small stone walls and meeting the occasional tourist, I arrive an hour past noon. I am plagued by hunger and thirst. Andi and Malte, with foresight, have already ordered the food. In a sun room, which has a very comfortable summer temperature, we enjoy our meal immensely. We are feeling so good, in fact, that we decide to continue today and climb the summit of Gokyo Ri. We have a waxing, near full moon, so we will have no problem if we have to descend late, in the dark. Andi takes his 16mm camera along, to film the last hours of the year on the summit.

It is good to have a 'simple' five-thousander with a technically easy ascent. It gives many tourists a chance to enjoy the magnificent panorama that unfolds on this 5,434 metre mountain. The view of four eight-thousanders alone is worth the effort. In closest proximity is Cho Oyu; Everest and Lhotse are neighbours and, further away in the east, Makalu, as well as the peaks of the seven-thousanders Pumo Ri, Gyachung Kang, Nuptse and Gauri Shankar.

Below lies a whole ocean of six-thousand-metre peaks. This late afternoon presents us with particularly beautiful scenery. Next to the pyramid of the Everest summit, from its western, Tibetan side, rises the light ball of the near full moon. Along with an American couple from Seattle, we absorb this hour in silence and meditation. I am infinitely grateful for the privilege to experience such moments in my life. Although it has cooled off considerably, we linger, observing the prayer flags fluttering in the dusk. Beyond, in all its magnificence, lies the top of the world.

We decide to stay in Gokyo for another day. The weather is good and we have extra time. The tranquillity up here is unparalleled. In the morning we take a leisurely walk to the fourth Gokyo lake, to look for the commemorative plaque for Reinhard Karl. Although we are searching with four people, we cannot find it. On the contrary, we actually lose sight of each other. All of a sudden, everyone has disappeared behind one hill or another. Originally, the plan was to walk to the Cho Oyu south wall. I call, but no one answers. So I just sit at the edge of the lake. Lost in thought, I throw stones onto the glistening ice. They glide over the ice, creating a long, monotonous sound, only sometimes interrupted by the eerie, fast travelling noise of the ice cracking somewhere.

Yesterday, I noticed the prominent peak of the Thorak Soso, behind Gokyo Ri. I mentioned to Malte that I would love to climb it. What shall I do with the rest of the day? I will just walk up there, casually, no pressure. I reach a grassy slope over big rocks. The ground is dry, sometimes frozen, occasionally thawed and muddy in the sun. I always have the mighty South Wall of Cho Oyu before my eyes, its close peak and huge snow plume. I can almost feel it on my face. Still, no one is in sight. Only after I reach the first saddle do I see two tiny figures far in the distance. I call and think I hear a reply; but I may be just imagining it; it is too windy to be certain. Towards the second saddle, I have to bypass or cross snowfields. Occasionally, I break through the snow, which is not deep but it is more work. The higher I climb, the colder it gets. I am wearing everything I have with me. I have brought neither food nor drink. Nevertheless, suddenly, nothing can keep me from climbing the peak of Thorak Soso. At 5,800 metres it is not particularly high in the face of the eight-thousanders, but the winds are getting tough. I grit my teeth. A few more metres, and I reach a ridge with loose flat stones. When I trip, they clink like layers of ice floes. As I climb higher, the west flank of Everest is gradually rising over the ridge; and suddenly, like a light golden ball, the moon rises at the eastern horizon. A sacred moment. If I had thought yesterday, that the hour on the summit was a highlight, this moment surpasses it. I simply stand in admiration and reverence. I am not a particularly religious person but, in moments like this, I feel a deep respect for nature.

I continue, step by step. Bigger boulders now require some light climbing. Getting higher and higher, I can see the snow-covered mountains around the Nang Pa La and further away, on the horizon, the ridge of Rolwaling with the 7,125 metre Gauri Shankar. The climbing is now of a more difficult degree, but a glance upwards assures me that it is not far to the summit. I can already see a *chorten* with prayer flags. It is two thirty in the afternoon of 28 December. An azure sky lies above me. A few more steps and I reach the *chorten* of the summit of Thorak Soso. I sit on my knapsack all by myself, and look around, a bit tired but very happy. The moon has climbed a little higher above the western flank of Everest. The prominent peak of Makalu, bathed in a blue-grey light, contrasts with the blue horizon. It is the nearby Cho Oyu that fascinates me the most. How I would love to climb it from the Tibetan side!

While I am sitting there, I let the year pass in review. It was

At the Thorak So So Peak.

a busy year. First there was the exhibition for the seventy-fifth anniversary of the Franz-Fischer-Hut in the Oberreintal, simultaneously the work on publications on the history of the Oberreintal and its host Franz Fischer. I purchased a farm in the Allgäu, my home country, with the idea of living there some time in the future, with family. And now, we are here, on a musical trek. Perhaps there is something here that will open new horizons for me — who knows. Of foremost importance, however, is to always have the courage for a new beginning.

I take a few photos, then descend slowly and carefully over the big boulders. As soon as I reach the terrain with grass and snow patches, I make better time. By the time I meet the path to the Cho Oyu South Wall, dusk has fallen around me. I am thirsty and hungry. My eyes adjust quickly to the moonlight and I find my way back to the houses of Gokyo without a problem. Suddenly, I think I hear a whistle, then I hear it again clearly. 'Charly,' someone calls. I know that it is not Andi or Malte. 'Yes, I'm here!' I answer.

'Here Tsewang and Manbir.' Moments later, they are next to me with a full thermos of tea. I am so grateful for their foresight. Later, at the lodge, among friends, a delicious pizza completes the day.

New Year's Eve

The year has come to its end. Yesterday, we descended in one stretch from Gokyo to Namche Bazar. We had a clear day, without a cloud in the sky.

The second Gokyo lake had invited us to another game of flicking stones, across its solid ice cover, clear as glass. We all sat there for half an hour, flicking stone after stone, following their long path, listening to the sound. For a moment we felt as if we had returned to our childhood, carefree and unobserved. Just the four of us, Andi, Malte, Tsewang and I, in this immense space of the Himalaya.

Today, we are part of the village scene of Namche Bazar. We are stuffing ourselves with cinnamon rolls, chocolate croissants and café au lait at Helmer's Bakery. Later, we try to call Germany, but all the lines are hopelessly busy. A later attempt fails as well. So we stroll through the picturesque streets with their souvenir shops, and haggle with the good-humoured Sherpa women over a few yak bells — partly for the sake of haggling. What else could we take? Our backpacks are already bursting.

In the evening we talk Gyaltsen into joining us for a game of billiards. He has never held a billiard cue in his hand before, and we get quite a kick out of his confusion, when he first takes aim at the multicoloured balls. Bob Marley is singing at the juke box, later John Lennon, Brian Adams and all the classics, which make us feel nostalgic in the gloomy light of the pool bar. Oh, why not have another whisky cola? It is Malte's turn to break the triangle of balls with the white one.

One ball, with a half ring, disappears with a plonk into the left corner pocket. Gyaltsen is in my team.

On the last day of the year, we rise to a foggy grey morning. Not a single mountain of the Himalayas can be seen. We have not had any bad weather since the snow at the Lamjura pass at Junbesi. Malte is up early. He wants to be sure to make it to Lukla in time to book our flights to Kathmandu and to find accommodation. He leaves the house, even before we are up. Through a haze we hear him say his goodbyes and thank yous. 'Until summer then, Gyaltsen. *Namaste.*'

A little later, Gyaltsen wakes us. Asman Tamang and Sheila, his eighteen-year-old kitchen help, join us for breakfast. She is an inconspicuous, fragile-looking girl with an infectious laugh, which makes one completely overlook the fact that she is cross-eyed. Asman and Sheila will help Andi and me to carry our loads today. The dulcimer, one guitar, the film camera case, the tripod, the heavy backpacks; everything has to go to Lukla today. Serki, Gyaltsen's daughter, prepares a delicious omelette and Tibetan bread for breakfast.

Once more we witness Gyaltsen's morning ritual. He pours fresh water into the ten silver bowls of his Buddha shrine, then lights some herbs in an incense vessel and solemnly walks it through the house, thus protecting it from evil spirits — all the time absorbed in his act, and chanting, *'Om mani padme hum'.* We feel greatly privileged to be included in this deeply religious ceremony; it has been an invaluable experience for us. *Om mani padme hum*, murmurs Gyaltsen again.

We say farewell in the grey, rock-paved courtyard of his house. Two big *dokos* are loaded. Asman has to carry my heavy dulcimer, Sheila the guitar, our sleeping bags and some small items. As I say goodbye to Gyaltsen's daughter, she hands me a little Tibetan yak bell. I liked Serki from the moment I saw her, and I am touched by this nice little gesture which shows a return of my sympathy. Once more, Gyaltsen drapes a *khata* around Andi's and my neck, also a symbol of gratitude and hope for good health and a reunion. *'Namaste*, Gyaltsen.' I feel tears swelling in my eyes. Involuntarily, my thoughts return to the scene when I first met Gyaltsen and his wife Gyalmo, in 1993, at this very spot, in front of their house.

I still puzzle over the coincidence — why did I walk into this particular house, six years ago, and not another? In Peter Matthiessen's book *The Snow Leopard*, I read of the Buddhist saying: 'When you are ready, your teacher will be there.' Gyaltsen has, in that Asian way of seeing things, become my teacher. His modesty and composure, even in stressful situations, and his serenity at the hut impress me anew every year.

As I thank him for the two wonderful weeks and, above all, his friendship, he strokes my face with his hand. Tashi, the little Tibetan dog, jumps up at Andi and me. *Namaste*, Gyaltsen, Serki, Tsewang and little Dawa. The gloomy day, with its low hanging clouds, is in sympathy with us, as we have to leave Gyaltsen's house and home, Namche Bazar.

At the *stupa*, we meet a few Tibetans who have collected firewood to warm their tents. *'Tashi delek*,' they greet us cheerfully.

Goodbye to Namche Bazaar.

We reach Lukla in the afternoon. The streets are grey and wet and the mud clings to our boots. The village is full of trekkers. Flights to Kathmandu are not possible. Andi and I are quite exhausted, but happy to have arrived. We had to take over some of Sheila's load because she had to stop several times, exhausted and dripping with sweat. Not that she would complain; her pride would not permit it. We regretted having given her such a heavy load.

Malte has reserved quarters in Sherpa Dawa's Himalaya Lodge. Thanks to Dawa, he could also arrange for three seats on a plane tomorrow morning.

Although fully booked, somehow he managed. Perhaps the reason is that he wants to work with Andi, who has the prospect of becoming the new guardian of the *Watzmann-Haus.** We are having *dal bhat* by the warm stove, as a farewell meal with Asman and Sheila. The two are giggling constantly. We cannot have a real conversation with them, because they do not speak any English. They are beaming with pleasure when we hand them their hard-earned wages; Sheila presses a surprise kiss on my cheek. This seems quite emancipated for a Tibetan girl and I love it! What a surprise at the close of the year. Asman and Sheila wave and disappear into the streets of Lukla. Farewells are, in my opinion, the moments which release the deepest emotions. Pain, loss, love, even hate, are always stronger in a moment of parting.

In the evening, Malte, Andi and I play our instruments just for fun and ourselves, but it turns out to be entertainment for the whole lodge. Andi has developed into a fine percussionist on our trip. The international crowd rewards us with big applause and Dawa sends us one whisky cola after another, perhaps, potentially, still with one eye on the Watzmann project. We feel slightly awkward about so much attention. We

---

* Lodge on the Watzmann, mountain in the eastern German Alps close to the Austrian border, above Berchtesgaden.

leave and move on, and find ourselves, at a late hour, in a little discotheque. Andi pays for a round. I cannot believe my eyes: is this really a Sherpani? Hard to believe.

A pretty girl in typical Sherpa clothes — black, heavy wool skirt with horizontally striped apron — is dancing to English rock music in the dim light of the disco. A curious sight for sure. Soon, all three of us hit the dance floor. A blue spotlight haunts the little bar, ghostlike; the teeth of the dancers are flashing white. In a mix of intoxication and life, I dance around the Sherpani to an oldie from the seventies. Life can be so *exhilarating!*

'What time is it, Andi?' 'Twenty past twelve already, Charly.' Without noticing it, we had slipped into a new year.

At Wanger's Home in Kathmandu

I hardly know Klaus Wanger, the current coordinator of the DAV Summit Club for Nepal travellers in Kathmandu. It was mainly through our telephone conversations about the aggregate, which, in the end, we did not need. I think that he and his wife Agathe smiled, benevolently, on our group of individualists when they first met us at the Dechenling Restaurant, before our trek. However, they thought the idea of the musical trek charming and when they had a chance to get to know each of us better, we got along very well.

Upon our return from the Khumbu, we are invited for dinner at their home in Patan. With a delicious Nepalese meal — rice with tofu, *dal bhat*, vegetables, chicken with pomegranate — we have an excellent French red wine. We exchange ideas and recount our adventures on the road. Agathe tells us, in lively conversation and with expertise, about religious and historical interconnections in the Kathmandu valley, the early reigns of the Gopala and Kirati, the Licchavi and Thakuri to the later Malla and Shah dynasties. In more detail, she describes the modern times of the Rana, up to the middle of the twentieth century, with their prime ministers, who are held in the same high rank and esteem as the kings.

Lastly, she briefly covers the current political situation of Nepal, its multiparty government and the constitutional functions of the king.

Normally, Agathe gives this kind of informative talk about political, religious, or cultural issues only in her capacity as a tour guide for Summit Club guests. We are lucky to benefit in this pleasant and exceptional way from her exceptional knowledge. Over a dessert of apple with yoghurt, Klaus wants to know about our plans for the next few days in Kathmandu. He has a few suggestions. 'How about a performance at Haatiban for the orphans of *Nepalhilfe Beilngries?*'[*]

'Hmm, not a bad idea. A few public performances in Kathmandu would raise the profile of our whole musical trek through Nepal,' I suggest to the group.

But Klaus and Agathe would like us to perform also in the royal city of Bhaktapur and in the classical Rana estate of Babar Mahal, which nowadays houses craft shops and cafés.

'Let's first play at Haatiban and see how it goes, then we will talk about the others.' I take over because I feel responsible for the technical and organisational aspect, while Erich does the musical part. I like the direct and uncomplicated manner in which Klaus arranges the necessary details. We have agreed on Tuesday afternoon in the garden of the Haatiban resort! It is about twenty kilometres outside Kathmandu.

We continue a lovely evening at Agathe's and Klaus' place. The red wine is delicious. Carolin, Erich and Beeker tell stories about their Stuttgart band, Andi and Ebi are talking 'business' — filming, while Malte and Simon leaf through some German newspapers that are lying about. I exchange a few experiences of previous mountaineering adventures with Klaus. Christoph, their five-year-old son, plays among all this with his Nepalese friend. Parvati, the Wangers' housekeeper and cook, who was responsible for the excellent dinner, serves coffee, while we are listening to the spheric saxophone music of the Norwegian Jan Garbarek and mystical flute tunes of the Indian, Hariprasad Chaurasia.

---

[*] Organization to help Nepalese orphans with shelter and education. Established in Beilngries, Bavaria.

Music for Orphans

Klaus has organised a minibus for us, for nine thirty in the morning. We have been standing in the street with our instruments, waiting, since nine o'clock. This street leads eastwards, away from the Thamel quarter, close to the new King's Palace and a little alley which is home to the Dechenling Garden Restaurant. Unfortunately, this is also the collection place for foul-smelling garbage. Piled up are mostly stinking plastic bags, fermenting fruit leftovers and half-empty, mouldy cans. The murky water of the disgusting-looking brown puddles at the edge of the pile offers a sad reflection of the morning sun. Dogs are scratching at the bags for leftovers. Several beggar women are warming themselves at a burning garbage pile. A shoeshine boy leaves the corner where he spent the night. Young men are hanging colourful Indian cotton clothes on a brick wall, which is painted over with advertisements.

Carolin and Erich are sitting on my dulcimer case, bored, smoking cigarettes. Andi, leaning against a black cast iron fence, reads the latest edition of the *Kathmandu Post*; Simon and Malte are squatting, half asleep, next to their guitars. We had a late night yesterday. Beeker and Ebi are haggling with a rug dealer on the other side of the street. I am close to blowing my stack because the bus, which is supposed to take us to the vicinity of the Haatiban, is nowhere to be seen. We have already walked around the circular drive, from which it is supposed to leave, several times. There is no bus in sight. My friends are starting to look at me very sceptically. 'I don't think it's going to work out,' says Carolin, slightly irritated, because she has been bothered by close to a hundred beggars by now. 'We could have slept for another hour!'

'I am sure that the Wangers are waiting with the children,' I try to pacify her.

I am a bit upset, not only at the pessimism of my friends, but the disinterest or lack of responsibility of the bus driver, also angers me. Gone is the Far Eastern composure when I take the telephone impatiently from the man behind the desk of the Dechenling restaurant. Indeed, the bus has left for Haatiban without us and Klaus has been waiting with the children for a while at Champadevi. 'Go, get your stuff, quick! We are taking a taxi!' I yell at them excitedly, in a commanding voice. We need three taxis to accommodate all of us and our equipment. We leave the smog of the city behind us as we pass by several villages. A picturesque road leads up to the village of Pharping, which is famous for its Vishnu temple. There are pools here with unusually clear water. It is therefore natural, that the women of Pharping wash their laundry mainly here in these pools.

In a dale, is the parking lot, where this old light-blue mini bus which was to have taken us there, should be. But there is no one to pick us up, not a single soul around. Eventually, a parking lot attendant emerges from behind a wooden blue shack. In a few English words, he attempts to explain to us that shortly a Land Rover from the resort will come down to pick us up. We settle down in a sunny spot, beside the parking area. It is much cooler in the shade. After all it is January. My anger has dissipated and the tension that was there between us a while ago has reverted to the usual friendly atmosphere. My instinct has proved me right. The Wangers would wait for us with the children. It would have been a terrible disappointment if we had given up.

Half an hour later, we find ourselves sitting on the white plastic chairs of the Haatiban Resort Hotel, which, like the

Dechenling Garden Restaurant, belongs to Phintso, the Bhutanese. It is mainly used by visitors from the DAV Summit Club. On a clear day, they can enjoy the spectacular view of the Rolwaling, Helambu and the Langtang Himalaya. Even the lowest of the eight-thousanders, Shishapangma, is visible from here.

We ask the hotel manager, a fortyish-year-old, chubby local man, for Klaus and his gang. 'They are on the way,' he tells us with a smile.

'How many children are there?' I want to know. 'About twenty. They should be back soon. Their lunch is ordered for one o'clock.' Then he disappears into the hotel again, a rustic, solid and cosy round structure.

Under a group of fir trees, chairs are arranged on a neatly groomed lawn; lunch is attractively displayed on three tables. There are potato chips, hamburgers, meatballs, potatoes, fresh carrots, cucumber, French fries, bread, tea and Coke. Only the children are missing. But they are already announcing their arrival with their happy loud voices coming from the forest, and now they are storming out of the wood, skipping and laughing. Apart from Klaus, Agathe, Christoph and Parvati the cook, there are three women as chaperones for the eighteen children. They are a mixed group of girls and boys, all nice-looking kids, clean and groomed, in clean clothes and decent shoes, in contrast with the street children of Kathmandu.

Where does one start and stop? There would be so many individually sad stories to tell of these orphans who were fortunate enough to have ended up in the care of Nepalhilfe Beilngries. These are the few children who, after the loss of their parents, have been lucky, compared to the many homeless children living in, for us, unimaginable poverty, in the cities of Nepal. It almost seems that these children here live in a glass house. They are completely detached from their past and, protected; having escaped misery, they now live in a seemingly wholesome world with the guidance of a school, and much less conflict.

A bit shy with us, but encouraged by their chaperones, they shake our hands. Looking around at my friends, I can see that they are all taken by these slightly reserved children's faces and the mysterious, dark eyes. We are tempted to hear about their life stories, but resist. It would not be nice to single out just a few. We will attempt to offer them an hour or two of fun.

It is not long before the tables are cleared of all food. Another piece of bread and a sip of Coke, and we start unpacking our instruments. The picnic tables are nearly depleted by now. The children are starting to take their seats in the half circle of chairs. There is a cloudless sky above; and beyond the far side of the valley rise the snow-white peaks of the Himalayas. Completely quiet now, the children are looking at us with anticipation. We can hear only the light whistling of the wind in the fir trees.

Erich gives the usual sign; the sequence of the pieces we play is more or less the same. Although it is the first time since Namche Bazar that we have played together, it goes really well. The children visibly enjoy our funny Bavarian pieces. It is quite possible that this is the first live concert for most of them. From the very beginning, Carolin and I agreed, that music should be the binding element of our trek, that our music should open the hearts of the people. We did not expect though, to have an opportunity to make a social contribution in the form of a concert for Nepalhilfe Beilngries. It makes us proud, especially since at home we know two members of this worthwhile organisation, which has an excellent reputation internationally. And we are grateful that Klaus Wanger organised this for us.

Erich not only leads the beat, he also is the one who tells the stories to the songs in English, and always with great charm. In my opinion, Erich, who has composed a lot of music, is a brilliant musician. Carolin, his partner, is not only a superb double bass player. She combines a strong social conscience with a healthy Swabian talent for business. They complement each other very well. It is nice to be included in their circle of friends.

One of the chaperones picks up Erich's texts and explains some details to the children. She does not have to say much for *Resham Firiri*, because it is so well known. If, until now, they have sat and listened quietly, the children become more animated with this song and are even humming along with it. The two verses take about five minutes — five intense minutes which are burned into our memory forever. Erich's restrained introduction is followed by my solo, which is taken over by Carolin with her tenor horn, then the refrain is played by both of us and the finale with all the instruments. This tune has enchanted us from the beginning.

Andi and Ebi are busy filming this afternoon's events. Unfortunately, Ebi has to fly home tomorrow for a prior filming engagement. During our trek I have learned to appreciate him, with his quiet and sensitive manner. Reflecting on how special our trip has been, I am overcome with sadness at the thought that we are about to separate.

When the attention span of the audience is challenged and people start to wiggle or yawn, it is time to stop. When children have to sit quietly for a long time, this is likely to happen. We play a last, slow Bavarian piece in 3/4 time, the *Mòrztaler*. Carolin loves this song. Although simple, it is warm and melancholic, yet dignified.

'One more *Resham Firiri*,' one of the girls requests, and then quickly one of the boys as well: 'One more!' It is so difficult to say no to them, so here we go, one more *Resham Firiri*.

It has become quite cool now. The instruments are beginning to sound off-key and my fingers are getting numb. It is time to end an unforgettable afternoon, which had such an unpromising beginning. While we are packing

up our instruments, the first children, with their chaperones, are starting to walk off towards the woods and down
to the bus. We take the rest of them in our midst and follow
behind.

The Newar

Ulrich Gruber

The Newar's represent an important part in the culture of the Himalayan kingdom; they cultivate ancient, highly developed, artistic traditions.

It is mainly due to them that we owe the presently existing, historical image of the settlements in the Kathmandu valley. Aside from the city's architecture, which is greatly admired by visitors, they have developed a highly differentiated, if sometimes confusing, social system. The Newars combine Mongolian and Indo-Aryan roots and use a Tibeto-Burmese language with their own Devanagari script, which is influenced by Sanskrit. They are certainly one of the oldest tribes of Nepal. It is said that Bodhisattva Manjushri himself settled them in the Kathmandu valley after draining the water from the old lake. Their complex social structure comprises city farmers, small landowners, craftsmen, merchants, architects, artists, scholars and priests, who follow Hinduism as well as Buddhism. Hindu priests of the Newars are called Deo Brahmin, the Buddhist ones Vajra Acharya. It is characteristic of Newari society, that the two main religions here have fused certain elements. Hindu gods and Buddhist shrines are equally celebrated with pujas (religious ceremonies).

Another remarkable institution of theirs is the *guthi*, city cooperatives, which regulate religious and social issues and administer temples in the cities of the Kathmandu valley. Kathmandu itself is today urbanised in the manner of western civilisation; pure traditional dresses are seldom seen. In Patan or Bhaktapur however, women still wear black saris with red edging; their wrists and ankles are richly tattooed. Men wear a white, tightly buttoned shirt with a waistband and a vest. They are Jyapus, city farmers, who represent a unique farming development in the Kathmandu valley. They live in the city, whereas their land lies outside.

The Newars have the most celebrations of all Nepalese people. They frequently congregate for mostly religious festivities in which an opulent meal is one of the main objectives. Usually they serve plenty of rice, buffalo meat, vegetables, pickles, yoghurt, as well as large quantities of *chang* and *rakshi*, which is a fermented grain drink, and clear schnapps. The wedding ritual deserves special mention. At the age of seven to nine, girls are symbolically married to a divine bel-fruit, which is perceived as an incarnation of Vishnu. This marriage with the divine being is insoluble, a fact that helps make her life easier should she be divorced or widowed, because, she is still married to Vishnu. In general, Newari women are known to be particularly independent and self-assured. After the wedding, the young woman takes her place in her husband's family and adjusts herself in the new environment.

Japanese Banner

Anke, the ninth member of our group, was to join us originally, as a journalist, from the very beginning of our trip. She will leave from Frankfurt today after her successful completion of a Master's degree in Japanese Studies and will meet up with us tomorrow afternoon. We regret that she cannot be with us tonight for our show at the Dechenling Restaurant. Instead, I have a surprise in store for her, to congratulate her in style. We plan to hang a large white banner, with Japanese characters, across the balcony of our hotel, saying something to the effect of 'Welcome to the Master of Japanese Studies'. It should not be a problem to find the material for a white banner. There is plenty of that in the 'fabric' street below the Thahity Tole. And among the many international trekkers in Kathmandu it should not be a problem to find a person capable of writing Japanese. Indeed, it is not! At the Pumpernickel café I ask a young Japanese if he would translate in writing the few words that I have written on a piece of paper. He looks at me in surprise and asks: 'What is it for?' 'For one of my friends. She just finished her Japanese Studies degree. 'Aha', the young man nods his head and starts writing.

I am in luck again. A tuk-tuk driver knows a man who paints car signs. This could be the right man for the task. I am told, that I will find his workshop at the end of Hunbahal Street, in the direction of Durbar Square. After lunch I set out, working my way through crowded streets, squeezing past rickshaws, roaming the fabric shops between Thahity Tole and Indra Chowk. Always accompanied by, 'You want change dollars? Hash? Marijuana? Very cheap!'

I proceed. Just ignore it! I have bad memories of my last black market deal in Varanasi in 1993, when several Indians tried to lure me into a side alley. I saw through their plan just in time. It may be that the black market exchange rate is better, but the risks are higher as well.

The Akash Bhairab temple lies on one of Kathmandu's main arteries. This is the heart of the metropolis. One can almost feel the pulse of the Old City. Here religious Hindus honour and touch the ubiquitous Ganesh altars. Ganesh, the elephant-headed son of Shiva, is the god of success and good luck.

Amid fabric and curtain shops, goldsmiths and antique dealers, the drivers of the colourfully painted rickshaws constantly ring their bells. 'Hello, Mister. Rickshaw? Very cheap.' I wonder how many times a driver has to use these same few words, before landing a fare, when he is on the road day-in, day-out, weaving through empty Coke bottles, baskets, cosmetics scents, rolled up rugs, vegetable stands, colourful piles of sweaters and ironed slacks.

Among the crowd is an old Newari in *sukuwal*, the low cut pants, and *iskot*, the Nepalese vest, carrying a heavy sack of rice, always hanging on to his *duku*. Nothing can disturb his determined path, not the signals of the motorbikes nor the tuk-tuks, nor the yelling of the various merchants. Just as undisturbed by the activity around him, is a bull, trotting along the street. The same goes for the grey cow further down, eating discarded vegetables from a white plastic pail.

Wooden houses of the ancient part of Kathmandu, with their artful balconies and windows, are now hidden behind un-stuccoed brick houses. Here and there one sees a building under construction or a ruined house. From the fifth floor, a woman is staring, with fixed eyes, at the busy street life below.

Laundry is drying on a line in the city smog. I am amazed at the variety of things one can see in one tiny area of this fascinating city. A group of men is sitting on plastic chairs in front of a restaurant, drinking tea. Elegant women in saris of the most diverse colours are strolling by. Next to a store with artistic *thangkas*, someone is selling plastic toilet brushes. On the opposite side, colourful crochet wool bikinis are for sale, as well as canvas bags and rice paper goods. Next door to them, a man is dusting CDs and cassettes.

I take all this in, then decide to ask an older man for Hunbahal Street.

'This way, this way. Where are you from?' he answers and asks at the same time. 'Germany,' I answer in a hurry, heading for the dark alley that leads south to Durbar Square. *'Namaste,'* he calls after me. Here, in the oldest Newari quarter of Kathmandu, it is quieter. No car traffic, no tuk-tuks, only a motorcycle occasionally rattles by. The Newar are not a homogenous group, but are united by language and cultural tradition. Tibetan and Indian influences create their own unique culture. This is particularly visible in their religion, which is a synthesis of Hindu, Buddhist and animistic elements. The typical architecture of the Newari, the multi-storey brick house with stable or shop on the first floor, is also found here.

It is a street of small, inconspicuous shops, which also serve their owners as a living area and bedroom. An Indian sits cross-legged on a mattress, studying the latest newspaper. He sells saris, pyjamas and maternity dresses. After business hours, he will pull down the iron shutters and stretch out on his mattress until the new day begins. Then he will roll up the shutters again and the cycle will continue, day-in and day-out. Across the street are mostly shops with inexpensive fashion jewellery for women, — *tika's* (Newari) or *bindi's* (Hindu), religious symbols, which in their modern form appear as decorative, iridescent stickers above the nose or on the forehead of girls and women. Aside from *tikas*, there is a variety of plastic jewellery like necklaces, earrings, bracelets, combs and more. It is a play of colours in the light of the modest shop lamp, blinking and shimmering, in contrast with the otherwise dim Hunbahal Street. A few plants and a skinny pipal tree are reaching for the sun in a courtyard. A young woman is standing at a window, half dreaming, half watching children, who are chasing a green ball. I look into a shop that backs on to a courtyard, in which a young man is dusting his scooter with the reverence due to a shrine. Some products of modern technology look absolutely grotesque around these centuries-old houses. I look at the shop and ask the owner what he sells.

'I sell umbrellas and treasures,' he answers politely in a deep sonorous voice.

I cannot help but smile at the strange combination.

'I think you are from Germany,' he guesses and then adds: 'Would you like a very good umbrella from Nepal?' I say no thanks, but would like to know how much a treasure is. 'The small one is cheaper and the bigger one is more expensive,' he explains, laughing. 'Sorry, mister, between fifty and a hundred dollars.'

'Thank you, mister. Have a good time and good business,' I respond politely.

When I step back into the dim alley, his friendly smile follows me. For a few moments, time appears to stand still at the Hunbahal alley, until I see a young man fumbling with radios and computers, at the next corner. Over there, a mother in a faded yellow sari, is taking her three children for a walk. The youngest one is tied to her back. Next to the spice dealer, a tailor's sewing machine is purring. Now the alley takes a turn and ends up in a main street, leading to Durbar Square. Fish and plucked chicken are sold at the curb on the right. The buyers do not seem to object to swarms of flies on the dead animals. Opposite the fish store, I recognise immediately my paint shop with the red and white numbers. This is where my banner shall be created. I am actually surprised that I found this shop, against all odds, and that someone knew of its existence.

A roughly thirty-year-old, wiry and industrious man is painting a license number on a tuk-tuk. Congenially, I greet him, *'Namaste.'*

'Namaste, Sir. Do you need something?'

'Yes, I do.' I pull the white fabric from my knapsack and show him the paper with the Japanese characters.

'I need the Japanese in this size. And in between, if possible, some flowers.'

'For tomorrow morning?'

'Yes.'

'Three hundred rupees, mister,' he says and takes the material to his workshop, which looks like a hollow cube, where half-empty cans of paint, licence plates, motorcycle tanks, along with an assortment of brushes, provide for very artistic surroundings. Colourful pictures of Shiva, Vishnu or Ganesh are also present. An oversized oil painting with palm trees in the sun leads me to believe that my painter either comes from the southern Indian Ocean area, or this was a crazy request like mine, never picked up. Baffled at the ease with which all this fell into place, I start my way back. Through lively streets, I rush toward the Shree Antu. A heavy rain shower transforms the dusty streets of Kathmandu into a sea of muddy puddles.

I should have bought this very good Nepalese umbrella after all.

Performance in the Dechenling

As I am entering the Shree Antu after having breakfast at the Pumpernickel, the telephone rings. It is Klaus Wanger, for me.

'Charly, how would you like to perform with your group tonight at the Dechenling Garden Restaurant?'

'What's the occasion?' I want to know.

'Phintso is having a party and, when I told him about you guys, he said it would be great if you could start the evening with your music, before the regular band comes on.'

'Well, yes, great idea!' I am quick to answer. 'Everybody is out for breakfast at the moment but, I think, for now I can say that we will come.'

'I will have to call you in the afternoon, though, to confirm. Thanks for thinking of us, Klaus.'

Despite a bad cold, I now feel in a fantastic mood. I think it is really nice that Klaus is so helpful and, casually, arranges things in such a way that it puts a cultural angle on our visit to Kathmandu. Too bad, that Malte is in such a bad shape. Something did not agree with his stomach. Weak and pale, he is fighting fever and shivering fits. Beeker and Simon, who went to the south of Nepal for a few days, of course, know nothing about this unscheduled, impromptu, performance tonight. I just hope that they will return on time, by bus, from Chitwan National Park.

Around noon, Erich, Carolin and Andi return from breakfast at one of those enchanting green garden restaurants in Thamel. Without much ado, I inform them of the Dechenling project and that I had agreed and how could we really say no. . . ? Erich and Carolin look a bit perplexed, but they know me well enough to know that I do not like to go back on my word. It is not that I have to have my way, but sometimes the occasion calls for an immediate decision. Andi is really excited. It is one of the last evenings of his vacation. On Sunday, he has to fly back to Munich because of professional obligations.

'And how are we going to play tonight? We are only three. Malte is sick. Beeker and Simon may not be back on time!' is Erich's sceptical reaction.

'If worst comes to worst, that is what we will have to do, but I hope that the two will return on time. I am convinced it will be an amazing evening!'

I am bubbling with anticipation and excitement.

'I'll go and call Chris and her friend. Perhaps they have time and would like to come over,' Andi interjects.

'Who are they, Chris and her friend?' I ask curiously.

'Don't you remember? The American couple from Seattle, the ones from Gokyo Ri. Perhaps they would like to come.'

'Oh, those,' I remark casually, as if disinterested. But, to be honest, I would like to see this nice couple again at our performance. Carolin, who has not said a word so far, finally puts in her three words: 'Der Herr Wehrle!' That's it. But I am happy. It is exactly what she always says when she particularly likes something I do, whether it was in the last few years at the hut, or here, in Nepal. Now I know that she likes the Dechenling idea. She likes it when there is a little excitement. And that pleases me, too. Although I am neither a talented public speaker nor a professional musician, I do like the adrenaline rush that precedes these performances. Whether it is stage fright or plain excitement — in either case, it is something that has always given my life intensity.

We spend the afternoon on the hotel terrace, reading, then we take a shower and generally make ourselves presentable for an elegant party. Beeker and Simon, thank God, arrive just in time. We are supposed to be there at half past seven.

We drag our instruments along the main street of Thamel. Now I know how heavy my dulcimer case, with content, is. How hard Tamang Chiete had to work for a mere 300 rupees a day! The tourists, the variety of stores and displays, galleries, carpet stores, rickshaws and tuk-tuks, along with the evening illumination, make for an interesting walk to the Dechenling Garden. The mystical Nepalese flute music, floating from the CD stores, contributes to the special ambience. It is music that belongs here. It was born here.

Again we pass the pile of garbage bags, where we had waited for our bus last Tuesday. The scene is similar. Women with their grubby children are trying to keep warm at the burning waste, next to someone who is preparing his quarter for the night, a worn blanket. But this time, darkness hides the worst of this poverty under its coat.

At the garden gate to the Dechenling, we merge into a completely different world. Here we see only good-looking young women and men, elderly, slightly greying, gentlemen with their wives; everyone is well dressed. One can see, at first glance, that they are wealthy. They belong to the high society of Kathmandu. The uneasy conscience we felt five minutes ago, is pushed aside. It is almost shocking, how fast we can repress our embarrassment. The guard at the gate, in uniform, enforces this separation. One does not wish to be disturbed! I wonder again and again about the passiveness with which the greater part of the population, which lives on an absolute minimum, accepts this obvious imbalance. Perhaps, there is no way out; perhaps, it is simply fate. This is the way one lives. Eastern philosophy, art of living, apathy or fatalism?

There are fireplaces all across the garden. Groups of guests are standing around them to keep warm, while the food is being grilled. A strong aroma of Indian curry meets us at the door to the restaurant. The Kathmandu Band arrives, five pleasant-looking local men, dressed casually, around thirty. One of them could be Bob Marley's twin brother, he has the same figure, face, the same beard and the same hairstyle. It is not difficult to see, that he likes himself in this role. The instrumentation consists of three guitars, percussion and synthesiser, along with the usual amplifier.

Phintso, the twenty-five-year old host, in leather jacket and fine black slacks, walks in. Phintso is being groomed by his father as 'crown prince' to his business. However, the likeable young man does not wear his wealth on the outside. Klaus and Agathe introduce us to him and to the other musicians. A few 'nice to meet you's' here and there, and we are accepted.

Aside from Mr Tulsi, Erich's Brahmin and musician friend, these are the first musicians we have met here in Nepal. There is no apprehension or jealousy; on the contrary, as guest musicians we are invited to supply the entertainment for the first hour of the evening with our own repertoire. Just as we are setting up our instruments, I notice a blonde woman enter the room. It is Chris, the American, unaccompanied. Her husband, unfortunately, has suddenly become ill.

Erich, proud of his band, taps the beat on the floor with his right foot. After the first few bars, the stage fright that had built up in the face of such a big audience has disappeared. The festive mood in this side room, off the main dining room, spurs us on from the very beginning. We play well together. It is too bad that Malte cannot be with us. After every third number we take a short break. We receive enthusiastic applause.

During the breaks, Erich and Carolin, as the professional musicians, are the ones who get involved in conversations with the local musicians. Several guests admire my dulcimer and ask if it is difficult to learn and would one not get confused with so many strings. 'It may look difficult, but I taught myself and only started at twenty-five, so I suppose, it cannot really be too difficult.' Patiently, I answer all kinds of questions.

Now it's time for the Nepali pieces. No one suspects that we have some native tunes in our repertoire. The audience immediately catches fire and sings along with *Resham Firiri*. Carolin earns extra applause for her solo. Even the second and third piece appeal greatly to the audience.

After a short pause and refreshments, we decide to end our performance with the *Bavarian*. Afterwards, I have to change, because I am completely soaked. All relaxed now and content, I feel on cloud nine. I am happy that Simon and Beeker came back just in time and could join us for the performance. I noticed that they drank nothing but water while we were playing. I suspect that they spent a long night at the bar. While we are still packing our instruments, the two have already disappeared.

The local band plays classics of the sixties and seventies in quick succession. The Beatles, Rolling Stones, Pink Floyd etc. We now have time to enjoy a delicious Indian menu. There is red wine, beer, whisky, whatever our heart desires. We can talk without having to lower our voices. The music is loud enough not to be affected by it. Then it is Bob Marley's turn. Quietly, he starts a song about Pokhara, the town on Phewa lake, in the foothills of Annapurna, his home. As the instruments join him one after the other, the song reaches a fuller sound. It culminates in great excitement as the audience is drawn in and sings along: 'Po – kha – ra! —— Po – kha – ra!' Too bad, that there is no cassette. 'Bob Marley' is in his element and *No woman, no cry*, quintessential Bob Marley, follows. These and more hits make the evening quite a success. From time to time, the applause takes on wild proportions, until suddenly, things settle down and become a bit more subdued. Conversation has become more noticeable now. Everyone is in the best of moods. Unfortunately, the wine has run out before I can toast the evening with Klaus and Agathe.

'I would like to thank both of you very much for everything you have done!'

'We enjoyed it. It gave us some excitement too, for a change . . . When are you coming back to Nepal?'

'Oh, I will stay for a bit. I still want to do the Annapurna Circuit with Beeker and Anke.'

'I'm sure it will be nice in January. No tourists. I was there in 1980. I would be a little afraid to go back, because it has probably changed quite a bit. But I hope you have a great time and good weather. And when you are back, I will cook another dinner for you.'

'Thanks, Agathe, I am looking forward to that already.'

The garden is almost empty. It is midnight, time to say good night.

'Thanks for the invitation Phintso.'

'You are welcome Charly, nice to meet you and your friends. I hope to see you again.'

The guard at the garden gate stands to attention as we wish him a good night. The ashes are still glowing at the garbage pile.

Concert in Bhaktapur
and Changu Narayan

Anke Schulze

Christmas 1998.

Every evening, before going to bed, I sit there with my guitar, listening to the cassette of the three Nepalese pieces. I am trying to play the chords which my guitar teacher arranged for me to accompany the unfamiliar songs. I am sitting here in Berlin, all alone, while the others, in Nepal, have just arrived at Namche Bazar, their musical trek destination. I would have loved to go along with them, but I had to prepare for the last exams, which paid off, because now I have done it and I am a master of Japanese Studies. Yes! At the beginning of January, I will fly out to meet them.

At first, the music sounds strange. Unknown instruments, different harmonies. Asian music, I find, becomes more beautiful and interesting the more often one hears it. I try to hear the music inside me, try to feel the curious rhythm. The Nepalese songs could hardly be more different from the Bavarian country songs; they are more complex but also more charming.

On 8 January, I fly to Kathmandu. When I arrive, the next day, Charly is waiting for me at the airport. We take a taxi to the hotel. While Charly gives a quick rundown of the events of the last month, I try to take in my first impressions. It is too much. I only hear half of Charly's story. I just have to look and look again. 'Wow, you have made it. You are in Nepal!'

The moment we arrive at the hotel courtyard, I notice a big white banner across the second floor balustrade, but don't really pay attention to it. It takes a moment to sink in and to realise that it has Japanese characters and represents a welcome for me, as well as congratulations from the whole gang. The banner is decorated with a garland of marigolds. Normally, this is customary for a farewell with family and friends or as an offer at a Hindu temple, like a birthday bouquet.

After the trek to Namche Bazar and various side trips, everyone is now assembled at the hotel. The mood is peculiar — boisterous and euphoric. For the others, I suppose, it is the entire experience of a month of trekking. For me it is the joy of seeing everyone again and to, finally, be free. No more university, no exams, at least not for a while; no problems to solve, just seven weeks of Nepal awaiting me. Seven weeks that I have been looking forward to for such a long time.

Walking through the inner city of Kathmandu in the afternoon, from Thamel towards Durbar Square, a stranger in this unfamiliar and so magically colourful world, I almost feel like an intruder. I want to absorb all these various impressions and lock them into my memory, the colourful saris of the women, the dresses of the Sherpanis with the striped pinafore, the many vegetable vendors with their offerings, in the street, on the bike or on their shoulders, the tiny shops of the meat vendors at the corner. There are no high-tech scales and the shops are not exactly clean and shiny. Almost everything is moved by manpower, either carried by hand or on the back. Life in the old town of Kathmandu is hard, but it radiates a certain fascination that I cannot elude. There are scenes which I am tempted to photograph, but I do not find the courage.

Two days later, on the road to Bhaktapur in overloaded taxis, I am terribly excited. Tulsi and Dependra, two Nepalese friends, as well as Agathe and Klaus, are with us. Sure, I am used to performing music for guests of the hut in the evenings. We always play the same pieces with which everyone is quite familiar. Here in Nepal however, I don't know what to expect.

The trip to Bhaktapur was Agathe's and Klaus' idea. It is supposed to be a beautiful old city. Unfortunately, we have to be content with imagining its beauty. Without a special permit, which costs a packet, we are not allowed in with our instruments. But, what the heck! We play anyway. At the gate to the inner city, where we immediately attract a crowd of curious people, puzzling over our dulcimer and double bass, we unpack, tune the instruments and take up our positions. The Bavarian pieces first. The noisy chatter dies down. The children in particular, seem to enjoy our music, which encourages us to go on playing. Some start singing along with the Nepalese songs that are built into our repertoire.

Although we hear a few calls for us to leave, we see from the reaction that the great majority of the audience enjoys our music. And so, after an hour, we happily pack up the instruments and drive to Changu Narayan, as an alternative, an afterthought of Klaus' and Agathe's. The day is just too nice to drive home yet. Changu Narayan lies north of Bhaktapur. It is the most important sacred site of Vishnu in the area. We drive by fields, brick factories, along a dusty road, up into the hills. Our destination is the Vishnu temple at the top of the mountain. We carry our instruments past the parking lot, up hundreds of steps, which are lined with small two-storey houses. Halfway up is a large fountain. Immediately, we are followed by a big crowd of children with runny noses, messy hair and surprisingly complex English knowledge. I have a vision of 'The Pied Piper of Hamelin.'

The whole complex of the Hindu temple impresses me. It

is the first such temple that I have seen and I am surprised to see that it also serves as living space, in fact, a living *room*. In the centre, stands a tall pagoda, surrounded by various figures of Vishnu and Shiva, and smaller temples. The structure is of red brick; all sides are adorned with richly carved wooden doors and beams. I am not certain why I am surprised; I did not expect such artful architecture.

The square is huge and sunny. Half naked children are running about, playing; a mother is sitting on the floor, de-licing a small child. A puppy with a dull and dirty coat is tripping about, clumsily, aimlessly. There is nothing here that remotely resembles the respect and reverence-demanding silence of, for instance, a Gothic cathedral. The thought occurs to me, that the people here *live* with their gods. In spite

Erich with his accordion at the concert.

Concert at Changu Narayan.

of that, we are not allowed to play music here either, that is, not without paying.

We decide to play below, at the fountain — an ideal stage. The fountain is flanked by an arcade on one side. This is the perfect setting for us. After a while, we are surrounded by local people, and soon what must be the whole of Changu Narayan is assembled. The situation reminds me a little of our music-making at the hut. There too, we were really just a tiny group, integrated into a larger picture, and I feel because of that we are, essentially, part of the whole, rather than something singular or special. Naturally, we cause quite a sensation; this does not happen here everyday. Why else would people flock here in such large numbers? They look interested and curious, and yet seem to accept it as natural, almost casually. It makes me feel secure and calm. They watch us and appear amused. Women come to the fountain to fetch water. Just as our concert was a spontaneous decision, the villagers come by spontaneously and stay while we are playing.

The day that started out with a minor disappointment,

finds a happy ending in Changu Narayan. The inhabitants like our music. *Resham Firiri* has to be repeated, naturally. We could not have wished for a finer finale to our music trek. For me, however, this last concert is only the beginning of a wonderful, magical time in Nepal. And it is a good beginning, because I can now feel some of the euphoria that I notice in the others, within myself. This excitement will travel with me all the time and will, in several encounters with Nepal and its people, grow even stronger.

Farewell

Once-upon-a-time, so the legend goes, a large lake without an outlet formed in the Kathmandu valley. In the western parts of this lake grew a lotus flower of the greatest purity. As it came to blossom, *Adi Buddha*, or *Swayambhu*, 'the one born of himself', revealed himself in the flower. During a pilgrimage, one day the Bodhisattva Manjushri came to the banks of the lake to honour Swayambhu. After he had walked around the lake three times, he took his divine sword and cut a gap into the mountains that dammed the waters. Thus he created the gorge of Chobar. Now the water could flow off to the south. Where the lotus flower bloomed, a big hill rose. Later, the *stupa* of Swayambhunath was erected on top of this hill. Soon Manjushri settled the fertile former lake bottom with people from the mountains, thus creating the village between the Swayambhunath hill and the temple of Gujeshwari, who is one of the representations of the wife of Shiva. The holy site of Gujeshwari is close to modern Pashupatinath.

It is on the hill of Swayambhunath, where I sit and gaze over the sea of lights that is Kathmandu. I came here following an impulse. Alone, I sit on a green painted wooden bench, dreaming. I think of my friends, all of you who have been part of this happy journey. Without you it would not have happened.

An old Buddhist monk sits down beside me. When I ask him whether he is Tibetan, he smiles and says yes, he is from Lhasa. His content smile is contagious and eases my melancholy.

An afternoon at Pashupatinath.

A sadhu (wise man), follower of the Hindu god Shiva.

I walk clockwise around the *stupa* and turn all the worn-out brown metal prayer wheels, as an expression of my thanks for the wonderful time. The prayer flags are stretched star-like, from the tip of the *stupa* to the outside walls of the temple. In the beam of halogen lights they glow even more intensely than during the day; the all-seeing eyes of Buddha seem clearer, and the golden ball which crowns the top of the *stupa* looks like the moon against the evening sky. For a while I remain on the steps to the prayer room of one of the southerly buildings and listen to the monks' monotonous recital of *mantras*, a chorus of deep voices. Unexpectedly, the atmosphere reminds me of the village of Bhandar with its white *stupa*, the prayer flags in the evening light and Carolin's bass solo *Summer Time*. Although it is cold, I suddenly feel warm inside. In the face of

A well-known figure, Dudha dhari Baba, so called because of his habit of consuming milk (*dudh*) only.

an old man walking around Swayambhunath turning the prayer wheels, I see Gyaltsen.

To the left sits a group of local people singing religious chants by candlelight; one of them plays a small harmonium. I remember the boy who played *Resham Firiri* on his simple flute. Slowly, I continue and arrive at a courtyard. The houses are dark except for some faintly lit windows. A little shop at the end of the alley is still open. In a shack without doors, on heavy wooden boards, lies an old woman under a quilt, as if she were waiting to die there.

I see the barefoot woman in the snow at Lamjura La pass, under her heavy load. A shack next door houses a gallery of faded Buddha pictures.

When I return to my green bench above Kathmandu, the moon has risen. Suddenly the night seems to fall upon me. I should be on my way home. Lost in thoughts, I descend the

The Musical Trek Group.
Standing left to right:
'Master Sherpa' Eberhard, Simon, Malte, Charly, Carolin, and Beeker
Sitting: Erich and Andi.

steep stone steps of the Swayambhunath temple. Below, leaning against a tree, is my bike. After an adventurous ride through the dimly lit suburbs of Kathmandu — my bicycle has no lights — I am back in teeming Thamel. A group of young Japanese at a street corner play American songs on their guitars. I listen to them for a while. I will have a last glass of wine in Pilgrims Book House, which has a cosy restaurant.

Special Thanks

In conclusion, I wish to thank all my friends, Ang Gyaltsen Sherpa, Carolin Schattenkirchner, Jochen 'Erich' Abel, Eberhard Niethammer, Andi Wipper, Matthias 'Beeker' Bauche, Malte Jochmann, Simon Neumann, and especially Anke Schulze, for the courage to carry out the idea of the musical trek and for making it the experience of a lifetime.

Our porters Chiete, Manpuri, Harka, Asman, Pemba and Tsewang also made a considerable contribution to our happy days in the Himalaya.

We are much indebted to Klaus Wanger and Agathe Schmiddunser, who not only gave us valuable assistance as Nepal coordinators of the DAV Summit Club in Kathmandu, but beyond their call of duty presented us with many a wonderful evening in Nepal.

We thank the following companies and organizations: Conrad Outdoors in Penzberg, DAV Summit Club in Munich, Deuter Rucksäcke in Augsburg, the double bass factory Michael Krahmer in Mittenwald, as well as the carpenter of the dulcimer case, Albert Steigenberger in Ohlstadt.

Anke Schulze has given me many hours of invaluable advice while at work on the manuscript. The many nights she spent on the computer were essential to this book. Furthermore, I thank Achim Pasold and Siggi Uttendörfer for the editing, as well my friends Friedemann Galm, Helmut Zebhauser, Wolfgang Opitz and Agathe Schmiddunser for the critical reading of the manuscript, Hubert Wehrs for the map of our trekking route, Günter Hess for the recording and cutting of the CD, and Jochen Abel for the advice on everything that had to do with music. I am very grateful to Dr Ulrich

Gruber for pointing out mistakes and errors in content and for the permission to use excerpts from his texts.

Glossary

Bhatti:	simple lodging or tea room.
Bodhisattva:	Term of Mahayana Buddhism, describing an enlightened one who remains on earth to help others to find redemption, thus sacrificing his own transcendence into *nirvana*.
Brahmin or Brahman	The highest of four castes of the Hindu, which comprises priests and scholars and enjoys certain privileges.
Chang:	Traditional beer made of grains of the Himalayan region.
Chapatti:	Thin flat bread made of a dough of flour and water and cooked on a flat pan called a *tawa*.
Chiya:	Milk tea.
Chorten:	Tibetan version of *stupa*.
DAV:	Deutscher Alpen-Verein – German Alpine Club.
Dal bhat:	General term for a Nepalese meal consisting of rice, lentils, vegetables (*tarkari*), and mixed pickles.
Dhoti:	A long piece of cloth worn by a man, wrap-around.
Djakri:	A person privileged by access to the spirits. Similar to the shaman of the North American native.
Dogma:	Traditional short walking stick of porters to rest their carrying basket on during short rests.

Doko:	Transport basket made of braided bamboo, to be carried on back.
Dudh:	Milk.
Duku:	Nepalese pointed hat for Hindu men.
Dzo:	Cross-breed of yak and cattle.
Geigenbau-Museum Mittenwald:	Violin Maker's Museum in Mittenwald, Bavaria.
Gompa:	Monastery; cloister of Tibetan Buddhism.
Istkot:	Nepalese vest.
Khata:	White cloth scarf or sash, exchanged as symbols of friendship on visits.
Khukri:	A Nepalese curved multipurpose knife.
Mandala:	Mystical diagram representing the dwelling of the god — in a circle framed by a square with four entrances. Used as aid for meditation in Hindu or Buddhist tradition.
Mani wall:	Long stone wall against which stone tablets with prayers are positioned, also used to rest against.
Mantra:	Mystical syllables, words or formulas, recited as prayers or for meditation.
Momo:	Stuffed dumplings made of dough, with a filling of vegetables or meat, similar to turnovers.
Nirvana:	The final goal of Buddhism, a transcendental state of a human being in which there is no more suffering, desire or, any claim or sense of an individual or self.
Nyingma-pa order:	Order of the Mahayana Buddhism whose lamas wear red hats, therefore also called 'Red Hats'.

Om mani padme hum:	Tibetan mantra meaning 'Oh jewel in the Lotus.'
Sadhu:	A wandering Hindu ascetic.
Stupa:	A sacred structure with bell shaped cupola, mostly built on sacred Buddhist relics.
Sukuwal:	Pants with low rise cut.
Thamel:	Tourist area of Kathmandu.
Thangka:	Tibetan painting on fabric, mostly with mandalas and images from the life of bodhisattvas, Gods and Buddhas.
Thukpa:	Popular noodle soup.
Tibetan Bread:	Thick and usually greasy flat bread made of flour and water.
Tuk-tuk:	Motorised tricycle used as a taxi.
Yak:	Longhaired, domesticated member of the buffalo family, mostly in the uplands of central Asia, kept as pack animal and for its milk and soft fur. Lives only at high altitudes.

References

Gruber, Ulrich. *Nepal, Ein Königreich im Schatten des Himalaya.* Prestel-Verlag: Munich, 1991.

Gruber, Ulrich. *Reiseföhrer Natur Nepal, Sikkim und Bhutan.* BLV Verlagsgesellschaft: Munich, 1995.

Uchide, Ryohei. *Everest Treck.* Verlag J. Berg: Munich, 1991.